What It Was Like...short stories of childhood memories of segregation in America

By
Lois Watkins

**What It Was Like...short stories of childhood
memories of segregation in America**
Copyright ©2016 Lois Watkins

ISBN 978-1506-901-22-0 PRINT
ISBN 978-1506-901-23-7 EBOOK

LCCN 2016930222

February 2016

Published and Distributed by
First Edition Design Publishing, Inc.
P.O. Box 20217, Sarasota, FL 34276-3217
www.firsteditiondesignpublishing.com

Acknowledgements

No one does it alone, ever.

To the inquisitive minds of the children of the Seattle School District, including those incarcerated in the Seattle & King County Juvenile Detention Center, the genesis of this project. Without you, this book would not exist.

To my coach, Eric Horsting. Oh, and his patience, perceptive mind and very deep well of knowledge.

My Aunt Margaret Tatum-Potter. Even at this stage in life nothing beats a good hand holding with love and encouragement, seeing more in me than I see in myself.

My "sun" Tony. My greatest gift, more than life itself!

Amun. Unconditional love.

Author's Note

This book is in no way meant to stand in the light of our heroes of the Civil Rights Movement.

The purpose of this book is to share my personal day-to-day experiences and impressions, through a series of short stories, of what is was like as a child growing up in a segregated America.

Table of Contents

INTRODUCTION

The America I grew up in from the 1940s to the late 1950s consisted primarily of black and white people. Black people were by far the largest minority group. It is now commonplace to see Asians and Hispanics in all areas throughout America, but they were practically nonexistent when I was growing up, with the exception of a few who lived in concentrated communities commonly referred to as barrios and Chinatown, usually located in America's coastal cities and our Southwestern border.

Imagine what it must have been like to have been a clearly visible minority surrounded by whites who restricted every part of your life. Black people were easily identified by their hair and skin color, so we stood out whenever we were out of place in a segregated America, which included all of America. Even though the South lawfully restricted lives of black Americans, the practice of discrimination in America was nationwide. We were allowed to live only in areas designated for us by whites, to attend all-black schools, and to sit only in areas set aside for us on public transportation, in movie theaters, restaurants, waiting rooms, and even public facilities such as restrooms. Segregation laws were so finely tuned to keep us in our place that we couldn't share even the same water fountains as whites. To violate the laws of segregation invited a violent response, and potentially death. Even as young children we were fully aware, and always knew to stay in our place.

While reading about my experiences living in a geographic area where segregation was the law (the South), please do not make the mistake of thinking the rest of America was as integrated as it is today, and that you could live and eat anywhere or go to any school that you either wanted or could afford. Segregation was not limited to the South; it was nationwide. Blacks could attend schools and access most public facilities without segregated seating and services in most areas other than the South, but blacks were still restricted to designated black neighborhoods as well as being limited to employment in service jobs in all of America. We were treated, at best, as though we were invisible, and depicted as low and degraded human beings at worst.

There were almost never images of anyone other than whites in movies, TV, magazines, children's textbooks, and billboards, which included all forms of advertisement. If you lived in a foreign country and these were your only sources of information about America, blacks would have been perceived as almost nonexistent. The rare exception when blacks were included consisted of scenes which included either black musicians, servants, or as lazy buffoons in movies who shuffled along, all of low intelligence. The same was true, but not to the extent of blacks, for the extremely rare portrayal of an Asian that you saw in the both very popular King Kong or Charlie Chan movies. Chan, the lead character who was played by a white actor and made up to appear Chinese, showed great intelligence and was very wise. All others who were Asian spoke broken English with one or two sentences.

We knew about Mexicans through Western movies. Their roles never went beyond being the leading man's sidekick or performing as an entertainer, with one or two token Latin Lovers thrown in. Mexicans held an advantage over blacks because actors like Cesar Romero and Anthony Quinn, who were Mexican actors, got integrated roles interacting with whites in an almost equal role. When I grew up in Los Angeles, California in the '50s, it was considered derogatory to refer to Mexicans as Mexican, which was akin to what we now refer to as the "N" word. They preferred being called Spanish. This was in spite of the fact that there were towns in the Southwest that prohibited Mexicans from accessing facilities, the same as with segregated blacks.

The majority of neighborhoods in America, like the South, were places where most racial minority groups lived in segregated communities. Asians lived primarily on the West Coast and in some areas of the North Atlantic. Most Asians, particularly Chinese, came to America to build its railroads and work in mines during the mid-18th Century. They suffered discrimination and abuse and were referred to as the "yellow peril" by whites in America. Hispanics lived mainly in the Southwest as well as the Pacific Coast and the North Atlantic, with Mexico bordering our southern border. There were some communities of both groups scattered in smaller numbers throughout the Midwest. If blacks who lived in areas other than the South where there were no segregation laws chose to move into an all-white neighborhood, it would create open and very violent hostilities toward them. Often blacks who moved into these neighborhoods were threatened by the Ku Klux Klan with cross burnings on their lawns, and even bombings. If the black person chose to stay and someone else sold a home to a black person, the entire neighborhood of whites would leave the area, most moving to the suburbs and leaving the inner cities to blacks and other minorities.

Malcom X's family, which lived in both Wisconsin and Michigan in his early years, received the same treatment as a black family in the South who actively rebelled against racism, leading to death and destruction with impunity. In concentrated areas of America, other minorities experienced racial segregation and discrimination as well, particularly Chinese, Japanese, and Mexicans, but never the same magnitude and length of time as blacks. Blacks experienced segregation as the next step up from enslavement for over two hundred fifty years in America.

Some Hispanics were able to cross the racial divide while still maintaining their identity with dignity. Cesar Romero is an example. Even though he was stereotyped as a Latin Lover, unlike black men he was allowed to be appealing to white women, and even touch them on screen. Contrast that with the 1957 movie *Island in the Sun*, directed by Robert Rossen, starring James Mason, Joan Fontaine, Joan Collins, Dorothy Dandridge, and Harry Belafonte. Dorothy Dandridge and Harry Belafonte were the two black actors in the movie. Harry Belafonte was allowed only to somewhat touch Joan Fontaine while assisting her in seating, while Dorothy Dandridge freely hugged and snuggled her white male lover. This movie was considered quite controversial because a black man and a white woman together on screen as potential lovers was considered taboo. There was never a hint of a kiss or signs of affection between them throughout the entire movie. The prohibition of black men and white women was reflective of racial attitudes in America, not just the South. In the South, a black man faced certain death if he were caught with a white woman for any reason other than to provide a service, certainly not friendship, and love was unthinkable. As a matter of fact, it was an unspoken rule in the South that black men, when around white women, looked down, never in the eyes of a white woman, so as to not offend or have their intentions misinterpreted. Their lives depended on it.

Discrimination in employment was nationwide in America. Other than seeing a doctor with a bag, it was extremely rare to see a black person carrying a briefcase. As a matter of fact, I have heard it discussed in my family as "You see that, and you wonder what he is carrying in there!" We weren't use to blacks having jobs that required a professional appearance beyond a principal, teacher, doctor, or lawyer--and nurses usually wore uniforms. Working in offices outside the black community was almost inconceivable.

In 1910, Southern states enacted new laws, forty-five years after the Civil War, commonly referred to as "Jim

Crow" laws. These were the laws that created the conditions under which I grew up during the first twelve years of my life. Segregation was legal. It became illegal for blacks and whites to share anything publicly for the next fifty years.

1

RACE-WHAT IT WAS ALL ABOUT

Hair- The Ritual -The black woman's untold ordeal that freed hair for everyone

I bit my bottom lip as I tightly pressed the top flap of my ear down protectively to avoid a direct burn. I winced as the intense heat from the smoking hot, heavy black steel straightening comb approached the side of my face to straighten my "bad" hair.

Sometimes the beautician would blow her breath to cool the side of my face as she approached my hair with the hot comb, but it was futile: nothing could protect me from the intense heat of the hot comb, which had just been removed from direct contact with an open flame. Each time she removed the comb from the flame, she would wipe it on a piece of cotton cloth before combing it through my hair, which she had parted into thin sections, each requiring her careful attention with the comb. If the comb scorched or burned the cloth when she removed it, it was gauged too hot, hot enough to burn my hair. The problem was solved immediately by blowing on the hot comb and finalizing the ritual by giving it a hissing touch with her spit-moisturized finger, and she would continue artfully twirling tufts of my hair around her finger in preparation for the next onslaught.

I had to learn quickly, at an early age, how to hold my head "right," and to calmly allow the beautician to go through my hair with the hot comb, section by section. If I didn't hold my head right and got burned, it was my fault, never the beautician's. I'd sometimes be admonished, "You gotta learn to hold your head right!"

It was a rite of passage for all little black girls in America to learn how to hold their head right, which included mastering two very important positions: how to hold the ear, and bending over far enough so that the beautician had access to the fine hairs that grew from the back of the neck. Holding the ear with the opposing side of your head resting awkwardly on your shoulder allowed the beautician unhindered access to all of the hair growing behind the ear. If you didn't take care to protect your ear by holding it down, you risked getting it burned. The final torture came when you were asked to bow your head to the point of having your chin rest uncomfortably on your chest, exposing the vulnerable short hairs on your neck so they could be straightened, the area we euphemistically referred to as "the kitchen." When this occurred, you froze, not moving nor flinching. The very worst reaction was to obey the natural instinct to move away from the heat and anticipated pain, to duck and dodge, even move a thirty-second of an inch. Any movement in this area, no matter how natural, invited a snap of pain from a quick burn. Bracing. The tension in the air became animate, all conversation ceased when the beautician got to this part of the hair-straightening ritual. Of all of the steps to having my hair straightened, having my kitchen straightened was the one most dreaded.

A popular term for getting your hair straightened was getting your hair "fried," and it was a true statement. As with frying anything, you must use oil and heat. The heat has to be hot enough to melt oil, as with frying food. Black women experienced the closest equivalent to having their hair fried when getting their hair straightened. The oil, usually Royal Crown, Dixie Peach, or Hair Rep, was applied to the hair before adding the heat of the straightening comb, which resulted in a good shiny, hard press. Sometimes the hot melting oil from the intense heat of the straightening comb would sizzle as it made direct contact with my scalp, and it would burn.

The sign of having had a good "hard press" was when the hair was so straight and stiff from the cooled oil that one could easily see your scalp as your hair hung in long straight spikes around your shoulders. The next phase was curling. Sometimes my hair would be so hot from the pressing with the straightening comb and pulling with the curling iron that I would have to sit for a while to allow it to cool before it could be curled. Having my hair curled with the curling irons was far less traumatic. It was the fun part of the whole process because I got the chance to focus on style, and the curling iron did not get as close to my scalp as a straightening comb.

I don't recall ever getting burned by curling irons except for those occasions when I felt that an overzealous beautician determined the straightening comb didn't get my hair straight enough before the curling and would do what was known as getting one's hair "pulled." This required that she go over each part of my already straightened hair with a curling iron, section by section, pulling my hair from the scalp to the ends. Since I don't believe curling irons were originally designed for this purpose, the frequent close intimacy to my scalp almost always assured several burns.

Black women were labeled "tender-headed" if they had difficulty getting their hair straightened. They would duck, dodge, and weave like a prize fighter at each wave of the hot comb. It didn't matter; there was no sympathy for the tender-headed black women. They were referred to with annoyance by beauticians, as it was unthinkable not to endure the process to keep the hair straightened. The tender-headed just had to get over it. The social pressure to maintain straightened hair far outweighed the pain associated with a visit to the local beautician. There were no exceptions. A black woman walking outside with her natural hair, even in the black community, would be shamed--it was unthinkable.

No matter how straight our hair after this ritual, if it

made contact with moisture of any kind, it went back to his natural state. Women who perspired through their scalps due to the close and intense heat had it worse because the heat of the iron would only exacerbate their condition, many times returning the hair to the original nappy state before the beautician could finish. The moisture from the sweating scalp sometimes created steam that burned the scalp as well. You risked a long-lasting sting if you attempted to straighten wet or moist hair.

*****

One beautician stands out in my mind because my sister, Carolyn, and I would privately cry when we were scheduled for our beauty appointment with Mrs. Tyler. As little girls, we felt we had no choice. She never quite dried our hair before applying the burning hot straightening comb to it. She was a divorced single mother rearing a small son and was extremely nervous, totally oblivious to the torture she so carelessly inflicted on our young heads. Looking back, I think Mrs. Tyler needed the money to make ends meet, and had just started a business without training or skills. We were children in the third and fifth grades, and our mother sent us rather than took us to see Mrs. Tyler. We were about eight and nine years old. All we knew was that a visit with Mrs. Tyler, no matter how good her end result, represented torture to us. We accepted the fact that we just had to go through it, we had to have our hair straightened, and this was a part of it. We could hear the hiss and see the smoke from the steam of our damp hair as we dug our nails into our palms with our small tightly-gripped fists, enduring the pain of the steam burn, praying it would end, even though each time it seemed to take forever. Luckily, our visits to Mrs. Tyler didn't last long; our mother noticed several burn spots on our scalps shortly after a visit. We were overjoyed that we never had to go back to Mrs. Tyler again. We were too young to grasp the reality that before or after Mrs. Tyler, the process always remained the same, only a little more merciful. Regardless, black girls and black women shared the same experiences with straightening their hair--nothing changed when you got older.   It was not at all uncommon to put a "warm" comb through a toddler's hair when she was beginning to show her first growth of natural black hair, thereby preparing her for a lifetime ritual. The expression would be, "I think she's about ready for me to start running a warm comb through her hair."

Black people divided their hair into two broad categories, "good" hair and "bad" hair. Black hair was considered good hair when it was, at worst, a tight wave, and, at best, straight. Natural black hair was classified as bad hair, and was considered nappy, frizzy, and kinky, difficult and sometimes painful to comb when dry, resulting in, at best, a puffy frizz if not straightened. We considered our natural hair an embarrassment, shameful, and a sign of an unkempt black woman. Black women went to great lengths to hide our natural hair. This attitude about black women's natural hair was shared among black women as well as black men. We considered our hair one of our least desirable physical traits; it made us stand out as different in a negative way, still a "wild" African. Straightening our hair made us more presentable and acceptable, less offensive, or so we thought. We shunned our natural hair, believing that to wear it that way was unthinkable, although we weren't more accepted by whites because of it. Maintaining straightened hair at all costs for black women was one of our attempts to get as close as possible to the white standard of beauty, and we enjoyed attempting to imitate the hair styles of white women.

Black women's desire to appear presentable to the white culture resulted in a black woman becoming the first self-made female millionaire in America, Madam C. J. Walker. Her efforts, as she described them, were not to straighten black women's hair, but for black women to "...take greater pride in their personal appearance," and to give their hair "proper attention." By addressing the hair needs of newly freed black women, by 1911, she had built the largest black manufacturing company in the world, Madam C. J. Walker Manufacturing Company in Indiana. Her business not only increased black women's self-esteem by providing opportunities for employment, it expanded black women's economic opportunities as well--they had job opportunities beyond share cropping, washing clothes and working as domestics for whites. She was a philanthropist for black causes and by her death in 1919, she had over 15,000 employees.

Like black churches, the black beauty shop was one of the centers of cultural exchange of information between black women in the black community. Getting your hair done usually took at least half a day, and sometimes all day. We would sit for hours gossiping and sharing what we knew of the up-to-date news and the latest in style and music. Black women would congregate, en masse, lined against the wall in various stages of getting their hair "done." This was especially true on Saturdays, the busiest time. We were preparing for one of the most important events of the week in the black community, attending church on Sunday.

Black beauty shops ranged from sitting at someone's kitchen stove, to a shop with a row of washing sinks and upright hair dryers, though there were few of the latter. A good beauty shop had the latest black magazines, Ebony, Jet, Sepia, and Bronze Thrills. We'd order from the local café and eat our meals at the beauty shop because the wait took so long to get our hair done and we didn't want to miss our turn. As with black churches, one of the biggest complaints about black beauticians was getting out on time.

The torture I've been describing was a commonplace ritual for over one hundred years for all black women in America whose hair was naturally nappy or very tightly curled. We were most ashamed and embarrassed by our hair in its natural state. We went through torturous lengths to have our hair appear as close to a white woman's as possible, hiding who we really were.

Black women before the '60s and the Civil Rights Movement knew being beautiful began with straightened hair. All media, including all black magazines, depicted only black females with straight hair--it was our unquestioned standard of beauty. Our naturally nappy hair was something to be hidden and quickly remedied. New growth, sometimes referred to as "edges," had to be quickly straightened when it occurred between appointments with your beautician. Every black woman's household had at least one straightening comb. It was okay to tell a friend, "Girl, you are going to have to do something about those edges...." It was accepted that your head would be sore for a few days after your hair had been straightened, and you had to be wary of your comb hooking onto a scab or two or three.

*****

Although black women had been routinely straightening their hair since the late 19th century, earlier black women who worked in the master's house during slavery would sometimes have to "iron" their hair to look presentable. My direct experience with this was during the '40s, '50s, and early '60s in America, the era before "black is beautiful," and before the Afro hairstyles which represented the sudden change in attitudes and images of blacks as a result of the Civil Rights Movement. For the first time in America, it became okay to just be black. It was not only okay to be black, it became okay to show off your natural hair with pride. This resulted in the ubiquitous large Afros of the '60s. Young black women throughout the nation suddenly, in droves, began to display their natural hair for the first time without shame or embarrassment. Not only did we proudly display our natural hair, we wore it big, unmistakable, difficult to ignore--the bigger the Afro, the better. Black men did the same. We proudly called our natural hair "Afros" because our hair unmistakably displayed our African roots.

We became united, presenting our true identity to America, not trying to be something other than what we were. We all knew we came from Africa--we didn't know where in Africa, but our evidence was our hair and skin color. We couldn't change our skin color, we had done our best with our hair and then it became okay, and we owned ourselves. This was the first time in America that American standards of beauty included black women, and most importantly, blacks became more accepting of standards of beauty for ourselves.

The shame of our natural hair had affected generations of black females, who never learned to swim for fear of getting their hair wet, returning it to the dreaded and embarrassing natural state as soon as it made contact with any moisture, including light humidity. I don't believe that other races of women have any idea of the lengths that black women went to in order to straighten their hair, nor do they understand the significance of the impact of freedom resulting from the Civil Rights Movement on our hair. The '60's gave us permission to accept all of ourselves, liberating black women from pain and suppression of their hair. We had over one hundred years of having to constantly suppress a natural part of ourselves, hating it. We accepted this as part of what black women must go through in order to look presentable and be accepted. We hid our natural hair at all costs. Some black men, particularly entertainers, would straighten their hair, which was referred to as "conking." They used chemicals such as lye instead of the torture of the hot comb, but most black men wore their hair naturally. Black men had only to allow their hair to grow longer for an Afro; black women had to develop new techniques for managing their hair in order to wear an Afro. I never questioned why black men freely wore their hair naturally, and black women were shamed by their natural hair and felt they couldn't. For black women, our hair was the only thing we could change to appear to fit in.

We started singing James Brown's song, "Say It Loud, I'm

Black and I'm Proud!" To other races this may have seemed overbearing, but to blacks, African-Americans, in over two hundred and fifty years in America, this was the first time in our history that it seemed okay to be black. We didn't feel less than anymore, and that whites were better than we were because of the way we looked. Black women stopped feeling the shame of their natural hair and showed their freedom and pride through their hair; we took it to heart. We allowed it to grow as large as possible, black women as well as men. The Afro started with young black women, and soon progressed to older black women who had at first criticized young black women for doing it.

The most positive outcome is that black women in America evolved to the place of personal choice. A lot of young black women today who have chosen to wear their hair naturally have no idea of what it was like to go through the full, old-fashioned, hair-straightening process. We now have a choice, and most importantly, all are accepted and no one cares. This is also true for white men--they were safe to wear long hair and pony tails, and they became hair-liberated as well. The 1967 off-Broadway musical "Hair" attests to the popular liberation through hair of the '60s.

What it meant to be called colored or Negro

My history professor at Langston University (a Traditionally Black College), Dr. Ada Lois Scipio, stated, "There are two things you can't be 'part' in America: 'part pregnant' or 'part black.'"

I don't care what you looked like, or if you were a combination of other races, as long as you had one drop of black blood you were considered Colored or Negro, as we were called at the time. The term used to describe us as black was considered derogatory until the Civil Rights movement of the '60s. Unlike today when people hyphenate their origins, such as African-American, Chinese-American,

Mexican-American etc., the rule of thumb was that black was black, there was no in between. This made things easy for segregation because there were mostly only blacks and whites in the South. With the exception of Chinese, Japanese, Mexicans and Puerto Ricans, the majority of other minority groups and cultures did not come to America until after the Civil Rights Movement.

To be black had a range of identifying characteristics. Blacks, even though considered of African descent, range in color from indistinguishable from white to ebony, which is why, I believe, we were referred to as colored. This convenience of classification ensured that no matter the mix, if you had black blood, no matter the percentage, you were black. African-American facial features range from appearing white, regardless of skin color, to the broad nose and thick lips associated with an African heritage. This range in physical characteristics can reveal itself in one black family. Black Americans are truly reflective of America's "melting pot."

As a result of so-called miscegenation, the common practice of interbreeding between races throughout slavery and post slavery, blacks were mixed with all cultures in America. Many blacks claim European and Native American ancestry as well as African. My grandmother, a mulatto, whose father was of German Jewish heritage, and her mother black, a direct descendent of house slaves from Haiti, always self-identified as black, without question. Some may find it amusing that I did not know this about my grandmother until I was an adult. I was a fourth generation from slavery--this was all I knew, I never questioned the fact that my grandmother had very light skin and long wavy hair and that we grandchildren would probably annoy her to no end by insisting that we "brush Gran Gran's hair." I didn't think anything at all of the fact that my mother was very light-skinned with hazel eyes, and some of her sisters and brothers were dark-skinned with brown eyes. I didn't notice these things as I grew up; we were all just black, Negro, colored. Regardless, we all suffered from the same circumstances during segregation. We knew with certainty that white people wouldn't take the time to distinguish between our shades, and were more focused on whether we held a trace of blackness, and if we did, we must know and stay in our place.

My father claimed a part Native American heritage, but we considered it a family joke. He was black, a Negro, regardless. I didn't take it seriously until I attended college in Oklahoma where some of my college friends joked about my "Indian" appearance, even though I denied it. It was considered somewhat disloyal for blacks to consider themselves to be anything other than black--we never really discussed what we were "mixed" with. I remember that one of my friends in college had an uncle they called "Uncle Chief." He looked Native American in every way, but self-identified as black, and no one questioned it.

The word "Negro" was our formal classification, and the term "colored" was how we were popularly referred to. Segregation signs designating our place commonly referred to us as colored. We did not consider either term, colored or Negro, to be degrading or insulting. The only term we reacted strongly to was the word "nigger." It is amazing to me that today's young blacks think it acceptable to distinguish between the terms "nigger," and "nigah," or "nigra," as white Southerners pronounced it. To me there is no difference. Yes, we would refer to each other using the term "nigger," as is done today, but it was never in public. It was unthinkable to use the term "nigger" openly, around white people. Using the term was an unspoken something we kept among ourselves. I think our young generation considers it degrading to be referred to as colored or Negro, and are okay with anyone referring to them as something we thought of as degrading and insulting during slavery and segregation.

During the Civil Rights Movement we began to refer to each other as "sister," "brother," or "bro." Even today, when describing racial identity when referring to blacks, even for non-blacks, it is still acceptable to refer to us as a sister or a brother. To me, the term implies mutual kinship and respect between blacks.

We all look like everything, except we have black blood. We are a great mixture of all colors, some of us indistinguishable from whites, but we were still all colored, Negroes. Those who could pass as white sometimes chose to do so. My grandmother, whose father was of German Jewish heritage, summed up the attitude of her generation when a white-appearing friend of mine who was proud to be black visited me. She said the following after my friend left: "My Lord! She doesn't know what an opportunity she is passing up!"

Blacks and other races – How we were portrayed during the '40s and '50s in America

I will never forget my first fleeting glimpse of an Asian. It was during a summer vacation with my aunts, uncles, and cousins in Oxnard, California. I stared blankly through the car window long after we had passed him, marveling at the fact that I had seen a real "Chinaman"! He had waved cheerily with a broad smile as the car honked when we passed what, to me, was an enigma.

This was less than ten years after the end of World War II. The Japanese population in America had been forcibly removed from their homes in California, Oregon, and Washington, the West Coast, where 80% lived, and placed in internment camps or what were referred to as "relocation camps" during World War II, when America was at war with Japan. They were confined to the camps and not free to go outside beyond the area that enclosed them. The camps were either surrounded by barbed wire or heavily wooded areas, and guard towers. There were seven states that housed ten camp locations; two were in Arkansas where I lived. This may explain why although there may have been Japanese in Arkansas during this time, I had never seen one before. There was not a trace of them outside the camps. My father spoke about passing a camp while on a train, when he worked for the railroad in Arkansas, wondering what the structure was all about. The relocation camps existed in America from 1942 to 1945. While the existence of the camps was only for a brief period, this blatant act of racism has had a lasting effect on the people and their culture in America. One must remember there were people of German and Italian ancestry in America who were not interned in concentration camps like the Japanese, even though we were at war with their countries as well.

I was eight years old, when I looked out of that car window and saw my first Asian. I didn't know if he was Chinese or Japanese, but everyone called him, "Choo Choo," and would wave and honk their horns whenever they saw him on the street. He would return with a wave and a smile as though he was the happiest person in the world.

Looking back, I think that was Choo Choo's way of coping with being a minority in America during the '40s through the '60s--smile all the time, appear happy to the public. Most importantly, don't appear to be a threat, sinister, or hostile--World War II had ended only seven years prior. I didn't know about these things; all I knew was that America had been at war with Japan and this was how they were depicted during the war. I had seen Asians in movies, particularly Charlie Chan movies, but Choo Choo was my first real one.

I remember seeing my first Hispanic; I was in the sixth grade. A Mexican family had suddenly moved into the black community in Little Rock, Arkansas, for the first time. Since there were only black and white people in Little Rock at the time, the black community was the only place the Mexican family was allowed to live. I assume that the powers that be did not consider them white enough to attend white schools, so a boy by the name of Richard Ramirez appeared at our school one day. We were advised by our teachers in hushed tones that a boy from Mexico would be attending our school. We were more curious than anything else to see what a real Mexican would look like. Luckily for Richard Ramirez, all the girls considered him extremely handsome, and the rest was history. He was readily accepted as one of us.

When I grew up in America there were primarily two races, black and white. Blacks were nine to ten percent of the population during the '40s--'50s. The 1870 Census was expanded to include Chinese, Native Americans, and East Asians, and during the '40s and '50s, they were less than one percent of the population in America. Hispanics, specifically Mexicans, weren't counted by the US Census nationwide until 1970, and were approximately 4.5% of the US population. It was rare to see other races in my region of the South. Quite frankly, I don't recall seeing any in Arkansas before the sixth grade. In America, unless you traveled to specific areas, such as Chinatowns and barrios in some major cities, you saw only white people and a few blacks, if any, depending on the area. There were no Chinatowns or barrios during this time when I grew up in Little Rock, the capital city of Arkansas.

Attitudes – Blacks toward whites and whites toward blacks

I don't remember when I learned about the lynching of black people. It was something that I seemed to always know that it existed. In my young mind, the lynching of blacks was an unspoken fear of the consequences for making white people mad.

During the times of slavery and segregation, hanging blacks was the preferred and most effective way of teaching us a lesson. Whites were not prosecuted for crimes against blacks, including murder. It was unthinkable to hold a white person accountable for a crime against blacks.

Entire white communities, including family picnics, would gather for the lynching of from one to several blacks at once. The last officially recorded lynching in America was in 1968. This was included as part of segregation; it was more than just separation of races. Blatant human injustices were condoned.

The period of Reconstruction after the Civil War, from 1867 to 1877, was the first step up from slavery for blacks. Attempts were made to establish segregated public schools for blacks, and other privileges, during this ten-year period. Provisions were made for providing education and other skills necessary for blacks to be successful as free people. It ended due to Southern opposition and northern withdrawal from the South, leaving the South to solve its own problems. This firmly established the governance of white supremacy and segregation in the South without northern interference. Blacks were left to the mercy of southern whites, their former oppressors. There were many poor whites in the South who were resentful of any privileges for blacks. Southern whites' attitudes toward blacks after slavery did not change because of the stroke of a pen. While most whites in the South could not afford to have plantations and own slaves, the Southern white culture fully supported it. Regardless of their economic status, whites considered themselves superior to blacks because, even though many were poor, they were white. Poor southern whites had only their color that made them superior to blacks, so they suppressed and brutalized blacks in order to clearly establish an unquestioning superiority of the white race. After Reconstruction, blacks were subjected to the same restraints during slavery, only this time they were officially free and their suppressors held black freedoms as underserving and in contempt! Blacks accepted this until the emergence of the Civil Rights Movement.

There were slave patrols prior to the Civil War, referred to by former slaves as "paddy rollers," but afterward, during Reconstruction, their numbers increased, and white groups formed the Ku Klux Klan, which generated Black Codes, and blacks lived in fear of being brutalized or lynched for the next one hundred years in America. Black Codes, established during Reconstruction, meant that blacks were put back in their place as much as possible. This became the white southern culture's way of managing the black population, through fear. In 1925, 40,000 members of the Ku Klux Klan marched in the streets of Washington, DC. They had established their presence beyond the segregated South. This was all a part of an effort to re-establish the dominance of whites and to return to antebellum slavery culture.

A strongly held belief by whites was that segregation was justified as "separate but equal," but whites held all of the power as well as wealth in America, and blacks were considered inferior and undeserving of a better life. Whites controlled everything, and blacks had nothing when they were freed from slavery. Everything had to be given to blacks, who, as former slaves, did not own property, nor had job skills beyond manual labor. A slave could not possess nor acquire anything that was not considered his master's. Many could not read or write, because it had been illegal in many places in the South to teach those skills to slaves. Being free, without education or assets, made blacks quite vulnerable to whites. They were dependent for basic survival upon the same whites who had fought and lost the Civil War.

There was great animosity toward newly freed blacks, and the whites, usually from the North, who tried to assist them during the period of Reconstruction, made Southern whites even more resentful. Blacks had to make a living within the constraints imposed upon them from the white world. Since blacks owned no land and had to work for whites who did own land, the white farmer held the land and needed workers, which resulted in freed slaves finding themselves working again as a different kind of slave, a sharecropper. Many blacks in the South were relegated to the position of sharecropper, still farming for their former masters for food and bare wages. Sharecroppers were dependent on their new masters for food and shelter, which was extended as credit. When it was time to pay, it was not at all unusual for the cost to exceed the monies earned through work. They seemed to never get out of debt, which resulted in a new form of slavery. There were white sharecroppers as well.

My father, who was quite precocious in math as a young child, told the story about his working in the cotton fields of Blytheville, Arkansas. He had the talent of being able to quickly tally the amounts owed to cotton pickers after they were officially weighed by the white farmer. The farmer soon learned about what my father, a little boy, was doing, and he quickly was sent off to be a water boy instead.

For blacks, a good job was a service job, and a job as postman and a black school principal or teacher at a black school were considered among the best. Others, such as an attorney, physician, or business owner, depended on the wealth of the black communities they served, because blacks were their only clients. Black women were relegated to being either teachers or nurses, or with fewer skills, a washerwoman, sharecropper, or a servant for whites.

White supremacy ruled the South after Reconstruction and its outgrowth, segregation, was an act of legal racism by whites who thought of themselves as superior and blacks inferior. Newly freed blacks were seen as an uncontrolled threat to white people's security, particularly white women. As a result, white southerners quickly devised the Black Codes laws to limit the freedoms of the newly emancipated slaves, a means to continue the custom of unequal treatment by creating laws of containment and restriction of their daily lives. By 1910, southern states had enacted new laws, commonly referred to as "Jim Crow" laws. These were the laws that created the conditions under which I grew up. Segregation was legal. It would be illegal for blacks and whites to share anything publicly for the next fifty years.

In today's world, many would assume that blacks during these times would have automatically retaliated against whites. We didn't. We were greatly outnumbered, and our lives depended on hiding our true feelings and knowing our place. We were former slaves who were quite familiar with the consequences of any hint of rebellion. Whites still held power over blacks, still controlling their lives. We made sure we stayed in our place, because not doing so could become a matter of being beaten or killed, to be used as an example to keep all others in their place. This practice was particularly true for black men. Blacks knew always to smile and agree with whites when in their presence. Blacks displayed their displeasure in passive-aggressive ways because it was safer. Popular depictions of slow walking, slow talking, and head-scratching black men who appeared to never fully understand what the condescending white man wanted were usually responding in a passive-aggressive manner, their way of safely rebelling. Black women were usually maids who never quite understood the complications of life experienced by the white world, but sometimes showed traces of mother wit. What whites didn't know at the time, but even I knew as a child, was that the "Ya'suh, boss" responses that blacks gave were insincere, and we spoke and lived as though there were two languages and two different worlds, which was true.

We would complain among ourselves. We knew that whites didn't expect much from us, we knew they considered us inferior, so we followed along. To become known as a "smart nigger," showing intelligence, gave hints of assuming equality and was not the smartest thing that a black could do. It could be interpreted as a threat, wanting to get out of line, out of place, the worst we could be perceived as doing.

In spite of this, my family's attitude toward racist name-calling was notable. My mother told the story about the starving, dirt-poor white girl who lived near my mother's home in Camden, Arkansas. This was during the Great Depression in the 1930s. The little girl was obviously starving. My mother's family of ten children invited her in to eat dinner. As she was eating, the family cat came near her food. When she saw the cat she yelled, "Scat, you nigger's cat!" My mother said that her father's immediate response to his children was to say, "Don't say or do anything; she doesn't know any better." He owned the only meat market in town that had a mostly white clientele, I am sure he practiced many moments of restraint.

I also remember a dinner conversation with my parents about germs. I couldn't have been older than seven when I laughingly said, trying to be funny, "Yeah, it's like having Germans all over you!" My parents quickly admonished me, saying, "Don't say that! It's impolite; you'll say something like that in front of company and embarrass us!" These were people who knew about slavery through direct connection with their slave ancestors who were still alive in their youth. Yet, they felt it was not okay to use derogatory terms about another race, including whites, at least publicly.

Black men were generally referred to as "boy" by whites if they did not know their names, and many times even if they did. The boy that they referred to could have been an actual boy, or someone a hundred years old; he would still be called boy by most white people and have to answer, usually, "Ya'suh, boss," or "Ya'suh, Mr...." It was explained to me that this was one of the reasons so many black men, my father and Martin Luther King, Jr. included, grew a mustache in order to show they were men, not boys. It didn't matter.

They were still called boy, and always responded when called. They knew that their lives depended on appearing to obey white people, and not showing a hint of displeasure or hostility.

Black survival depended on knowing the American white culture well, especially in the segregated South. We saw white women as fragile, helpless, and unable to do anything on their own. The image of the southern white female was one to which all blacks showed deference, whether she was deserving or not, and to do so was considered a sign of a good upbringing, showing you had good manners. One could surmise that this was part of what remained of the antebellum South and its veneration of white females, holding on to an image of white women from a bygone era. Black men were especially vulnerable when it came to white women. Most avoided being in their presence. When they were, eye contact was avoided at any cost by looking downward whenever speaking to her to avoid insulting her or having his intentions misunderstood. A black man's life depended on it.

A black youth from Chicago named Emmett Till, was visiting relatives in Mississippi during the summer. It is said that he either whistled or said something flirty to a white woman. He was fifteen years old when a group of white men took him out of bed late at night and beat him to death and then shot him because of his interaction with the white woman. I clearly remember his murder as one of the most traumatic experiences of my childhood. No one was ever punished, which wasn't surprising at the time.

I lived in the city, where most blacks' exposure to whites was through cleaning their homes, or having them in charge of parts of our daily lives like the local grocery store, insurance salesmen and collectors, milkmen, and everywhere downtown. If a white man came to our neighborhood for anything other than the usual occupations, it was a sign of something serious. Everyone who saw him would watch with suspicion, and wonder why he was there. White men represented authority and power. We considered them rich--or certainly all were living better than blacks. A white man's orders were to be obeyed without question, as during slavery. They wielded power over blacks, with severe consequences whenever we were perceived as being out of place.

Our survival depended greatly on our knowing our place and staying in it. This included our environment, as well as our attitude and behaviors. From young children to senior citizens, we all knew our place and stayed in it.

2

PUBLIC PERCEPTIONS

PUBLIC TRANSPORTATION

Bus riding etiquette

As soon as the white woman began her saunter down the aisle, I got up immediately without thinking to give her my seat, as any black person would do. It was a sure sign of manners and good home training, to make your parents proud. I proudly immediately gave up my seat. It was expected by all that I do this, children first. All of the white seats had been taken and I was seated near the side door opening, which clearly distinguished the separation of the colored section from the white one.

The white section of the bus extended from the front of the bus to the middle where the side door opened. The section for blacks, referred to as the "colored section," was from the seats behind the middle side door to the long bench-like seat that extended the width of the bus in the back. The side door provided enough distance between the races to keep everyone comfortable in their places. In case you were unsure where you should sit, as with everything where blacks and whites intersected, there was a boldly printed sign above the driver's windshield for all to see, providing clear and simple direction.

In addition to the signage, there was an unspoken protocol, but understood by all, as to how seating would be managed. If the colored section was filled to capacity and the white section was empty, or had available seats, blacks had to stand and remain in their section of the bus until seating became available in the colored section. Under no condition were we allowed to ever sit in the white section of the bus. If the white section became full as well as the colored section, blacks had to immediately give up their seats to white women as well as men if they were standing and a black person was seated--it's just the way things were. Under no circumstances could a white person be left standing if there were blacks seated.

These were the conditions under which Rosa Parks took her famous stand that was the beginning of the Montgomery Bus Boycott and the beginning of Martin Luther King's Civil Rights career. Imagine her frustration at having to give up her seat after a long day's work, and the indignity of having to give up her seat solely because she was black and a white person needed a seat. To the post-segregation reader, this is an obvious injustice. However, I ask the reader to consider two facts. One, this was one of our first steps up from slavery. Vestiges of the slave mindset of being respectful to white people were reflective of good manners and good parenting. Whites had not changed their attitudes toward blacks because slavery had ended; as a matter of fact, many were resentful. Every privilege, including riding public transportation, was given grudgingly. To cross the established racial lines during segregation could have proven fatal for blacks.

I don't remember my older sister being with me on the bus, but she must have been because of my young age. I would not have been traveling alone. She must have given up her seat as well, for two reasons: home training implied automatic respect shown to white people, and most importantly, my sister would have been sitting next to me. If I had been the only one to give up my seat, this would have left a seat vacant next to a black person, child or not. It didn't matter; under no circumstances were blacks and whites to sit next to each other, ever. Besides, a white person would not want to be that close to a black person.

Cabs

Black communities had black cabs that serviced the black community. I think my parents had to get a cab from Ninth Street, the black business section of Little Rock. Needless to say, I don't recall seeing a white cab driver in the black neighborhood. That's not to say there weren't any, but I don't recall seeing one, ever.

Cars

As in all communities, blacks owned cars and drove in black neighborhoods and on public highways. However, I recall rare summer Sunday afternoon drives to the exclusive white part of town, Pulaski Heights, where my Uncle Walter delivered mail as a postman. We were four adults and two children with faces pasted to the car windows, wide-eyed, marveling at the big beautiful two-story and ranch-style houses with magnificent lawns. I am sure the car packed with gawking blacks stood out like a sore thumb. Those summer Sunday afternoon drives were a way of cooling off from the Arkansas summer heat. I don't remember any problems riding around in the white neighborhood. It could have been because my uncle was well-known and well-liked, especially by children and dogs on his postal route. I remember white children waving to my uncle as we drove by, saying to others, "There goes Walter!" It was okay for white children to call all blacks, regardless of age or status, by their first name. A white child, or any white for that matter, would never address a black adult as Mr. or Mrs. Conversely, it was a sign of disrespect if a black child called any adult, black or white, by any name that was not preceded with Miss, Mrs., or Mr. It was a sign of respect whites never afforded blacks. The term Ms. had not been created.

I believe that one of the reasons that my uncle held the

job as a postman was because he had served in America's segregated army during WWII. I was told once that he was a part of the black cleanup crew, as with black men during the Civil War, who were charged with disposing of the dead after a very famous battle. I don't remember who told me this, but I clearly remember them adding and he never talked about it except once when he mentioned stepping over mounds of bodies. He was the most kind and gentle man. He was especially kind and generous to us, his nieces and nephews. All children were immediately attracted to him, I suspect he found consolation in the innocence of youth.

Media and Entertainment

Blacks and Other Minorities – The American media of the '40s, '50s, and '60s

If you visited America during times before the '60s and early '70s and watched movies, TV, listened to the radio, and read mainstream magazines and newspapers, you would seriously question the existence of blacks and other minorities. We were invisible. We were treated as though we didn't exist in the mainstream, with the exception of assuming roles of demeaning portrayals of ourselves. That was the only way our presence was acceptable in the media. We saw only white people in the media nationwide. In old movies you will notice that there isn't a trace of anything other than white people, even walking as extras in the background on streets in big cities like New York. Everyone was white.

Blacks saw themselves in their own publications, the most popular being *Ebony* and *Jet* magazines, published by the black-owned Johnson Publication Company. We also made our own films with all black actors through black writers, movie producers, and directors, commonly referred to as "race films." The major writer, producer and director of race films was Oscar Micheaux, who made more than forty movies. They were shown in the local black theaters and movie houses. These were the early venues for famous black entertainers who were formerly stars of stage and later to become known both nationally as well as internationally.

There were whites who imitated blacks, usually in comedic ways, depicting buffoonery with black faces, rolling big white eyes, big white or red lips, and speaking in the most ignorant tones. It was an accepted part of society and a carryover from the days of minstrel shows and vaudeville, where blacks were routinely depicted this way. Some black actors made themselves up in black face during these times as well.

Not unlike our mainstream media today, these were forms of entertainment that shaped and influenced our attitudes toward minorities--blacks in particular, because we were the largest minority population. It is insulting to blacks' history in America when we see a lot of the scenes in movies where blacks were disparaged have been reissued, and many of the scenes I describe have been removed, including cartoons like *Tom & Jerry* that depicted the black maid with huge feet wearing sloppy house shoes as slow and ignorant for comedic purposes. This is a part of American history and representative of generations of acceptable behaviors of whites toward minorities in America. To erase it softens white America's display of approved racism during these times, and makes it appear as though it never happened, when in fact it did. Routinely depicting blacks as well as other minorities in disparaging images was a common practice and was socially acceptable throughout the nation.

The 1927 Academy Award winning movie, *The Jazz Singer*, the first feature-length movie, featured a white man of Jewish ancestry, Al Jolson, in black face. In 1998, this 1927 movie was voted by the American Film Institute as one of the best American films of all time.

Amos 'n' Andy, a very popular radio and later a TV show, had white men, Freeman Gosden and Charlres Correll, portraying black men on radio, and switched to black men, Alvin Childress and Spencer Williams, when it became a TV program from 1951-53, and became a series of syndicated reruns from 1954-66. The program setting was always in Harlem, New York City's black community, and depicted blacks in generally accepted negative stereotypical ways for humor. One thing that stands out in my mind is the fact that the lead character, Amos, had a wife named Sapphire. As a result, throughout the length of this program, radio and TV, black women were negatively referred to as Sapphire. We didn't like it.

I remember as a child watching a parade that ended with two white men sitting on the back of a flatbed truck in black face and big white lips, playing slapstick with each other. I later heard my mother on the phone talking about it. She was very angry, but I was too young to understand what the fuss was about. I had seen this many times before in magazines, movies and TV, this was the way things were.

National Geographic magazine, for over one hundred years, has freely displayed the bare breasts of primitive black and South American women, as well as full frontal nudity of the men. This practice started in 1896, and sadly, the magazine has continued with its practice of freely displaying nudity of tribal minorities to this day. Never has *National Geographic* displayed a picture of a bare-breasted white woman, nor a full frontal nude picture of white man in the history of the publication. On those rare occasions when white female nudity is inferred, it is viewed from the back. A full frontal nude white male is viewed with genitals either blacked out or strategically hidden.

The TV Phone Tree

As soon as my mother hung up the phone it would ring again. Ringa ringa, ringa, it rang again and again, until the performance ended. Everyone in our community was so excited they could barely contain themselves. Seeing a black person on TV was akin to the Mars Rover landing and being greeted by a space alien. In the early '50s, the few black people who had TVs would call everyone they knew, yelling over the phone, "There's a colored man on TV!" This was done, unabashed, without a greeting, hanging up without a goodbye, and continuing with the calling tree unabated. We especially looked forward to the Ed Sullivan Show on Sunday nights. It was a variety show that would occasionally feature a famous black entertainer, and the phone tree would start as soon as it was announced.

This was during the era when families had one phone, no computer or texting, and only one TV, if any. The black person we were excited about seeing on TV was in all likelihood an entertainer, usually a famous singer or musician. We didn't have to figure out which channel to dial; there was only one. Seeing anyone black on TV was a rarity. There were no blacks in TV commercials, nor were there black news anchors, or game show hosts. Everyone was white, and all entertainment was geared toward entertainment reflective of white culture preferences.

We were the first in our neighborhood to get a TV. There was only one TV station that came from Memphis, Tennessee. TV wasn't on all day, mostly in the afternoon, ending, at the latest, around ten o'clock at night. Before and after the programming there would be what we called "snow," a gray, grainy, static- sounding screen. The closer it got to the time for TV programs to start, a "test pattern" would appear. The test pattern was a screen that had multiple shades of grey with circles and line drawings. I remember that one of the drawings was the head of an

Indian chief. We were so fascinated with TV that we would sometimes leave it on with the test pattern and grainy-sounding noises until the actual programming began. Neighbors would come from everywhere to watch, some sitting on the floor while others peered from outside through the living room window. Seeing a black person on TV, viewing this rarity first hand, made it all worth it. At school the next day, we would still be excited over the previous night's entertainment. It would be the talk of the school. The conversation always included detailed reenactments, with imitators using pencils or rulers as substitutes for handheld mics.

TV was in black and white. Retailers sold a rainbow striped plastic sheeting to cover the screen, to make it appear a facsimile of color TV. It didn't; it just showed colored stripes on a black, gray and white screen. This fad didn't last long because we had Technicolor in movies and knew full well what to expect from color TV.

Blacks looked horrible on TV--their faces always appeared ashen. Dry skin is more apparent on dark skin because dry skin, no matter the color, ends in light- colored flakes, giving the appearance of being ashy, or having a white dry haze to the skin. The irony was that in all likelihood blacks didn't have dry skin, they just looked ashy on TV because TV makeup artists hadn't perfected makeup coloring to match the coloring of dark skin. We would joke about it, but we were just so glad to have seen a black person on TV.

By the time I was in the sixth grade, on Friday's after school there was a local TV program called *Pat's Party*. It was normally a local all-white children's after-school program, but occasionally black children would be allowed on at random separate Friday shows. I don't recall there ever being a regular schedule for blacks. It seems the black schools were called at the last minute as a possible filler, and the teachers quickly rose to the occasion. We were a hastily gathered group of their smartest students for the show. Blacks always felt the need to show their best. This must have been before parent permission slips because everything happened in one day, from the notification to the performance. After a very brief rehearsal I sang the song, "He," made popular by the black song artist Al Hibbler, with my cousin Gloria, but I didn't really know how to sing. I was probably out of tune.

The arrangement with the program *Pat's Party* was not unusual. We look at programs like this to be reflective of segregation in the South, but nationwide programs, such as, *Dick Clark's American Bandstand* had regularly scheduled dates for black participation in Philadelphia where the program began. The separation of blacks on *American Bandstand* persisted in spite of the fact that they featured leading black entertainment artists, and the dancers on the set were still all white until 1964, when the program moved from Philadelphia to Los Angeles.

Minorities and the movies

I climbed the narrow and winding stairs to the colored section of the Nabor movie theater, holding my favorite uncle's hand, anticipating a wonderful movie after having assured him that I would not go to sleep and he have to carry me home this time. I felt that we were better off than whites, because, like most blacks, I believed during segregation that sitting so far away from the movie screen was better for our eyes. It was healthier, so we thought--we wouldn't have as many eye problems as whites who sat so close to the screen. The local movie theater had generously restricted black seating to the balcony. The balcony extended to less than half the length of the theater, limiting seating availability for black viewing.

Library of Congress, Prints and Photographs Division, Washington, DC

There was one all-black theater, called the Gem Theater, on Ninth Street in Little Rock, but I don't remember ever going there as a child.

As with all things during segregation, movies had their own unique way. The Charlie Chan movies during the 1930s were about a wise Chinese detective who solved many complicated murder cases. Charlie Chan was the lead character. Charlie Chan was portrayed by white actors, for twenty-two films, with makeup to appear Chinese. No one seemed to have a problem with the fact that a white person wore makeup to appear Asian while the rest of the characters portraying his family were clearly Asian. The same is true for the 1937 movie *The Good Earth*, a movie about Chinese farmers and their struggles during a famine. The main characters, Paul Muni and Louise Rainer, were white and made to appear Asian. It was inconceivable to have anyone other than a white person to play the leading role except in all black "Race Films," which were shown only in the black community with an all-black audience.

The Native Americans we saw in Cowboy and Indian (the

popular term for Native Americans) movies were mostly white extras wearing wigs and makeup to darken their skin to appear Native American. For generations, white boys as well as black boys played the game of Cowboys and Indians. It was a prized Christmas gift for a boy to get a cowboy hat, boots, and two toy six-shooters with a holster. The object of the game was to put loud caps in the guns and have a shootout, and mostly have the cowboys win over the Indians; they were America's heroes, the good guys. As with blacks and Mexicans, Native Americans could be killed with impunity. One famous western radio (1933) and later TV and movie character(1949-1957), The Lone Ranger, is reputed to have been inspired by the adventures of a black US Marshal, Bass Reeves, a former slave living in the eastern Oklahoma and Arkansas Indian Territory during the late 1800s. This information was not discussed openly until around 2013. The most recent Lone Ranger movie (starring Johnny Depp, 2013), may have contributed to this revelation; the lead character, however, The Lone Ranger, is still portrayed as a white man.

Print Media

Black people had their own magazines. The most popular black magazines were *Jet*, *Ebony*, *Sepia*, and *Bronze Thrills* for the teen girls. They could usually be found in someone's home or lying around in a black barber or beauty shop. This was the way we learned the news about blacks in America. *Jet* and *Ebony* were the most popular. One of the most jarring experiences of my childhood was when I opened the latest *Jet* magazine and saw the picture of a beaten to death, Emmett Till. *Bronze Thrills* was exactly what the name said--black stories about love and heartbreak, which I was too young to fully understand and appreciate.

Black Theatre

Our theatre consisted of famous black entertainers traveling throughout Southern routes known as the "Chittlin' Circuit." Black performers performed in black theaters in the South as well as other black communities throughout America. Local black communities, as in Little Rock, Arkansas, produced plays featuring famous black actors as well as local entertainment. I remember going to all-black plays and fashion shows at the Robinson Auditorium with my parents. This was an all-black audience that had its own standards of humor and criteria for good entertainment, and we enjoyed it fully without whites. My lasting impression was that this was where important things happened. My father once played the lead role of Barabbas in an Easter play at the theatre. Barabbas was a notorious prisoner during biblical times who was chosen to be released by the crowd and to have Jesus crucified. My parents rehearsed my father's lines repeatedly, and I am left with one line from the play that my mother repeated to him for many years, with many meanings, long after the play had ended: "Someday, Barabbas!" And those words could have been said for all blacks in American media.

3
CHANGING THE STORY--REVISIONISM

Revisionism: Changing history. Glossing over or rewriting unpleasant parts of history.

In my opinion, there are no better examples of efforts to change unpleasant parts of American history than the movies. What I find most interesting is that many of those who are revising history through depiction of segregation were adults, and had experienced it firsthand. One must conclude that efforts to revise the history of segregation through media are not omissions through ignorance, being unaware of its existence, but are deliberate. This is an insult to the people who are alive today and suffered the degradation of it. Basically, it invalidates our very real life experiences, and implies that things were not as bad as we say we experienced them.

My first experience with revisionism caught me off guard; I wasn't prepared for it. It was the movie *Pearl Harbor* (2001, directed by Michael Bay, written by Randall Wallace, starring Ben Affleck and Kate Beckinsale). I almost went into shock. I learned in one scene the full meaning of the word "revisionism." I felt it so deeply that I couldn't focus on the rest of the movie. There was one scene that distracted me from focusing on the rest of the movie because it kept replaying over and over, as though on a loop in my mind.

The movie's portrayal of the treatment of black men in the United States military during World War II caused a knee-jerk primitive reaction to the core of my soul. This was unexpected; I was completely caught off guard. I spontaneously fought for breath after exhaling with an audible gasp. I became mechanically fixated on the screen--I couldn't turn away. I would occasionally, involuntarily, shake my head with my hand to my mouth to muffle the uncontrollable, guttural sobs of hurt and disbelief. I was too fixated to just get up and walk out. There was also a dark and curious part of me that wanted to know if there were other scenes like this. Just how far did they go? And the looming unanswered question was why they chose to do this, to create a new false reality for the masses who probably are too young to remember or weren't born yet, and trust and rely on mass media to tell the story for them.

The scene that I will never forget was the movie's depiction of a full Navy crew, blacks and whites standing together, saluting the American flag on the bow of a ship at Pearl Harbor in 1941. The reality was that all of the US military were segregated, and blacks would have not have been allowed in the same area as whites, much less standing next to them saluting the flag as equals. Black soldiers were segregated, and confined to areas of the ship away from white soldiers. Everything on the ship was segregated, even their meals. I couldn't help but recall Evelio Grillo's description of his experience in a segregated troop as a black Hispanic man crossing on an American ship destined for India in the Pacific Ocean during World War II. In his book *Black Cuban, Black American*, (Arte P'ublico Press, Houston, Texas, 2000),_he details his experiences while crossing on the *U.S.S. Santa Paula*, "After fourteen hours of waiting in line along a wall of the wharf..."

> *"When it was our turn to board the gray, ghostly behemoth, we moved in single file along the gangplank, onto the vessel, and into the hold, the very bottom of the ship. Narrow little sleeping pads awaited us, arranged in stacks of three against both bulkheads.*
>
> *In the center, rows of triple bunks were arranged to account for every inch of space, while providing narrow aisles for maneuvering between the rows of bunks.*

There wasn't a single opening to daylight. We slept below the water line. We could hear the ocean slap constantly against the side of the ship. No forced air ventilation could match the stench cooked up by the sweat, the farts, and the vomit of two hundred men. This was only one of the many indignities inflicted upon us by the complement of white officers who commanded us.

White troops had fresh water for showering. Black troops had to shower with sea water. White troops had the ample stern of the ship to lounge during the day. Black troops were consigned to the narrow bow, so loaded with gear that it was difficult to find comfortable resting places. The sea sloshed over the bow furiously in foul weather, so even that area was unavailable to us when the sea thrashed. At such times we roamed the decks open to black troops until it was our turn to go into the dining halls -- for segregated meals.

The vast majority of men were confined to the foul-smelling hold.... We craved the fresh air of the open sea, available only when the bow was not awash with water.

Over the next few days, as we familiarized ourselves with the ship, we realized that the arrangements made for us were grossly discriminatory. We were infuriated and depressed, and we felt impotent."

As with the ship crossings of the Atlantic during the slave trade, (16th through 19th centuries), from Africa to the Caribbean and America, slaves were packed in the hold of the ship, row upon row, so were black soldiers during World War II. The only difference between the two was that the World War II troops weren't chained and they had sleeping pads.

At the time, the only thing I could think of to rationalize this inaccurate portrayal of American history was to think that to the writers, directors, and producers of the movie, my true black American experience was of little or of no significance. It was something easily tossed aside. Long afterward, I had another theory--black Americans' history in America is revised because of embarrassment and an effort to save face. Watching this movie was one of the rare times in my life that I just wanted to punch something, but I didn't know who or what to punch.

President Harry Truman signed Executive Order 9981 in 1948, ending the segregation of American troops. However, World War II had already ended in 1945, and in spite of his executive order, the last black troop in America did not end until 1954, six years after the executive order was signed, and nine years after the end of World War II.

With rare exceptions, such as the Tuskegee Airmen, blacks were assigned labor-intensive and dangerous jobs as stevedores who loaded military equipment for white soldiers. An example of the level of dangerous jobs assigned to black soldiers was the Port Chicago Mutiny incident in San Pedro, California, July 17, 1944. Black men had been relegated to loading and transporting bombs, shells, and torpedoes without having received prior training in handling of munitions. They were pressured to increase the daily quota of munitions loaded each day. An explosion on the shipyard resulted in 332 deaths and 390 injuries. The black troops responded to the tragedy by refusing to continue handling munitions. The Navy's response was to convict them of mutiny and to court-martial 208 of the men. It wasn't until 1990 that the Navy fully exonerated them.

Black men volunteered to fight in the Spanish Civil War (1936-1938) for the freedoms of other peoples, while returning home and not enjoying the same freedoms in America--blacks who during World Wars I and II volunteered to prove themselves as equal and just as patriotic as whites. Blacks experienced greater freedoms in a war-torn Europe during WW II than they had experienced in America. When they came home it was to segregation, business as usual, still not entitled to America's Constitutional freedoms, including, for many blacks in the South, the basic right to vote. Yet, the movie *Pearl Harbor* depicted blacks and whites standing together as though the degrading conditions blacks were subjected to throughout the military had during these times never existed.

Hyde Park

Another example of revisionism is the 2012 movie *Hyde Park on the Hudson*, written by Richard Nelson and directed by Roger Mitchell. Throughout the movie, interior scenes of the White House show an all-white wait staff, with the exception of one lone black male waiter.

The 1997 television miniseries *My Thirty Years Back Stairs at the White House*, based loosely on the book by Lillian Rogers Parks and collaborator, Frances Spatz, depicts the generations of black servants who served presidents and first ladies, as maids, waiters, butlers, etc. Servant jobs were performed by a fully integrated staff in the White House throughout. The White House paid separate salaries to black servants, which was less than white servants' pay. In their book, they quote a famous scene between Eleanor Roosevelt, the First Lady of the White House, under President Franklin Roosevelt's administration, and her mother-in-law:

"When the mother of Franklin D. Roosevelt arrived at the White House, she stood around and saw a White House staff of black people doing the housework, saying, 'You should have white people like we do at home.' Eleanor Roosevelt responded, 'Mother, I have never told you this before, but I must tell you now, you run your household, and I'll run mine!'"

These were considered jobs that black people did,

especially in the segregated South where blacks were freed slaves. In the South, we believed that a white person was either an immigrant or extremely poor to do the work traditionally done by blacks. It should be noted that in other areas of America, these duties were performed by newly arrived immigrants as well as other minorities.

Flags of Our Fathers

The movie *Flags of Our Fathers* (2006), a movie written by William Broyles, Jr. and Paul Haggis, and co-produced and directed by Clint Eastwood, depicts the WW II story of the Battle of Iwo Jima, and the aftermath of the lives of the soldiers depicted on a statue in Washington, DC, of the same name. What stood out to me in the movie was one scene where the lead characters were disembarking from a train. As soon as the train reached its station and began to slow down to a stop, a long row of white porters dressed in sparkly white uniforms jumped off to assist the passengers. I blinked--I couldn't believe what I had just witnessed. Before my eyes, within my lifetime, was a glaring effort to revise black and American history and to invalidate my life experiences of what I knew to be true.

Seeing this revision of American history was particularly painful to me because it denied the existence of a very important, hard-fought period in America. The Sleeping Car Porter's Union, founded by a black man named A. Phillip Randolph, was a very rare and powerful black union for all service jobs on railroads, from cook to sleeping car porters. All were black, with possibly a few rare exceptions. These were considered good jobs for black men, among the best that they could get. Any movies of interior scenes on American trains from the beginning of movies to the '70s, including the movie *Silver Streak* (1976), written by Colin Higgins, directed by Arthur Hiller, and starring Gene Wilder,

Jill Clayburgh, and Richard Pryor, accurately depicted an all-black staff with the exception of the conductor. That's just the way it was.

The historical omission in *Flags of Our Fathers* is particularly distressing when you realize that the co-producer and director, Clint Eastwood, made another movie in the same year about a WWII battle with Japan on the island of Iwo Jima (*Letters from Iwo Jima*, 2006) where he went through great lengths to ensure the authenticity of the depiction of the Japanese and the Japanese culture. He was commended by the Japanese for his efforts and a supplementary documentary of the movie was made about his efforts. However, this causes me to question the reason for the omission of American history in *Flags of Our Fathers.* Clint Eastwood was an adult in America during segregation--he must have known about it. The omission could not have been due to ignorance.

The revision of the experience of segregation in America is to discount its existence and to downplay its significance while invalidating the feelings of black people who experienced it for generations, to assuage the guilt of those in most of America who enforced and condoned it. Segregation was the next step away from slavery, the next level in which our country allowed us to live. Revisionism make it seem as though my true life experiences were fantasies I created, that my feelings about the abuses are unwarranted, but old newsreels, photographs, and an abundance of old movies make it real. This is a significant part of American history, and the truth should never be forgotten. Since most minorities during the era of segregation were depicted in disparaging ways, it seems only right and just to begin healing by accurately portraying history, if for no other reason than to show how our times have truly changed. What was commonplace then would be unthinkable today.

4

SEGREGATION ABERRATIONS – THINGS THAT WEREN'T SUPPOSED TO HAPPEN

A general rule was that blacks lived on the black side of town, and whites lived in the white section, except in a few unusual situations. I'll call these "segregation aberrations" because, as with most things in life, even during post slavery and segregation, not every circumstance fit into a nice tidy box. Things happened that weren't supposed to happen.

Annette

Annette was our playmate for a summer who lived closest to our house with bordering backyards. She had the misfortune of being an extremely lonely little white girl in the black community. She was part of a straggly and questionable white family consisting of her mother, Annette, and her toddler brother Paul. I recall the haze of a white man who would come around infrequently. This was significant because, as far as I can remember, white people lived far away from black people. We seldom saw them in the black community, except for those who came on business. We would mostly see whites when we went downtown, away from the black community. Our community, as I understood it, was always all black, except for this brief period of having one white family.

While Annette's family lived within the vast sea of the black community, I believe they were all but ignored except by my older sister, Carolyn, and me. Annette and her mother must have been extremely poor to live among us, even for a short time, especially since she was a white woman living mostly alone with young children in a black neighborhood.

Looking back, no matter how temporary Annette and her mother's stay, they must have been in dire circumstances to have their choices limited to living among blacks.

Annette was one of the loneliest children I can recall from my childhood. My sister and I were her only playmates, and weren't always available; we each had many other friends. Annette didn't seem to have any. We interacted only when we saw each other and it was convenient for both sides.

In spite of her loneliness and willingness to play at any cost, there were rules, and the rules were always in place. My sister and I were not allowed on their property, and her mother forbade her on ours. I remember once running quickly to her back door to retrieve a ball that had strayed. We were restricted to playing where our property lines met, and we couldn't play together at all when the hazily remembered white man and his male friends were around. As a matter of fact, we were completely ignored by Annette when they were there, as she admitted to us, she had been instructed to behave this way by her mother.

Sometimes Annette would yell out her back door as we stood at the property line waiting for her to come outside to play, not daring to move closer: "My mama said I can't play with y'all today!" It didn't bother us; we understood why. We accepted it and life went on. Poor or not, at least Annette and her mother had their color and could live anywhere they chose and could afford; their stay in our neighborhood was temporary. We were indifferent to her staying or leaving.

My Father--The Black "Student Prince"

The weary vacuum cleaner salesman was out of breath and overloaded with the burden of carrying his vacuum cleaner door to door for miles in the heat of an Arkansas summer sun. He trudged wearily with determination and the remaining dregs of optimism to the front door of the expansive mansion unfolding before him. He gathered the last of his sun-melted confidence and brushed past the insignificant black boy mowing the lawn on the Cockrells' estate. He paused for a moment as he wiped his fatigued face with an overused and tobacco-stained country rag, completely ignoring the black boy's unsolicited outburst. The thought of a black boy admonishing him, a white man, "We don't need no vacuum cleaners here!" He thought with indignation, didn't the boy know that it wasn't his place to tell a white man what to do? The white salesman had not asked him a question, and he resented highly the out of place admonishment from a lowly black boy trying to tell him what to do. He continued his weary trek along the endlessly long and winding path to the imposing entrance to the mansion.

Walter Watkins, Watkins Private Collection

He always began his day with high hopes of making a sale, but his panting from the weariness of the heat and fading hope betrayed itself through his tired and half-hearted efforts at ringing the doorbell. He tried to maintain a sense of dignity while straightening his long-ago wilted tie, an impossibly false sense of freshness, while balancing the many parts of the vacuum cleaner like a gangly octopus. The reward for his efforts was the very brief experience of the relief of the shade of the front porch.

He didn't have to wait long for an answer. As soon as he rang the doorbell, the door opened immediately to reveal the owner of the mansion, Ashley Cockrell. She quickly stuck her head through the door and pointed to the black boy still mowing the lawn, admonishing the salesman to, "Ask him!"

The black boy's mowing continued unabated as though he hadn't heard Mrs. Cockrell's admonishment to the salesman, he knew his place and carefully contained his private sense of victory. He had heard Mrs. Cockrell's voice, which was clearly and loudly directed toward him, more so than at the salesman. The salesman was weary, enraged, and traumatized by the ultimate humiliation by the upper class of his own kind, a wealthy white woman, directing him to the lowest of the low. He was momentarily confused as to where best to direct his rage. He did his best with what was left of his dignity to manage the parts of his trade as he began the humiliating trek down the now familiar undulating path from the Cockrell mansion. As he neared the end of the pathway, he eyed the mowing black boy and expressed his rage as he paused, harked deeply, and spat on the freshly cut green grass and turn to continue his journey. The brown bubbles from his tobacco-stained spit would soon evaporate in the hot sun, but one thing was assured: the memories of this incident would never go away. The two men would remember this incident for the rest of their lives. The words "We don't need no vacuum cleaners here!" And the deep impact of the admonishment to "Ask him!" would never be forgotten by either of them, but for different reasons.

The black boy mowing the lawn was my father, Walter Watkins. He had managed to graduate from high school in spite of the fact that the high school that his small black community had sacrificed for and built on their own had been burned to the ground by the Ku Klux Klan the night it was completed. He had risen from the burned-out ashes and hopes of a new high school to graduate and enroll in Philander Smith College, a traditionally black college, in Little Rock, Arkansas. The self-described poor but honest country boy had left the dusty cotton producing fields of Blytheville, Arkansas, with high hopes and no money, and the desire to attend college.

My father got a job working in the kitchen of the Cockrell estate shortly after his arrival in Little Rock. The Cockrells were a very wealthy old Arkansas family who lived, I was told by my father, in a thirty-room mansion. After working for them for three months, which included tutoring their children in math, the family matriarch, Ashley Cockrell, decided to support all of my father's expenses throughout his college years. Not only did he have all of his college years paid for, this country boy from Blytheville now lived in the carriage house above the garage on the mansion grounds. He had his own keys to the wine cellar and liquor cabinets to access any time he wanted. Almost overnight, he became the big man on campus, the "Fratman," in the Alpha Phi Alpha Fraternity, the oldest black fraternity in America. He was allowed to do pretty much what he wanted on campus because this was during the Great Depression of the 1930s, the college needed full-tuition, cash-paying students, and black students who could afford this, like my father, were a rarity. Luckily he was smart and got good grades in spite of it all. My father was firmly established as a member of the Cockrell family for the rest of their lives. Until he died at the age of ninety-two, my father always made it a point to visit them until the last remaining Cockrell of his generation died.

The Cockrells never knew this, but their influence on my father had a lasting effect, and on his children as well. While both my parents were good cooks, especially Southern comfort foods, all of our meals required the whole family eat together with full formal place settings at the table, eating dinner at the same time every day, and proper table manners were always the rule of the day. My parents' dinner menus are, in my opinion, reflective of their hopes and aspirations for our future. I will never forget the one time my parents fed us a tomato aspic salad. It was awful! I can remember only one other time it was served, and that was for the two of them to enjoy. But woe unto you if you stood between me and a Sunday dinner of curried chicken and rice. Imagine, in the Deep South, having this for a Sunday dinner instead of fried chicken. After I left home I didn't get another whiff of the wonderful fragrance of curry until I was in college, where the wife of a visiting professor from India would occasionally fill the hallways with the aroma of curry. I loved it--at the first whiff I would immediately begin reminiscing about my favorite Sunday childhood dinner.

These were during times when segregation and mistreatment of blacks was legal, and whites were allowed to abuse blacks with impunity. The Cockrells, even though they didn't have to, showed my father their generosity beyond his imagination. Most importantly, it didn't stop with my father; it was passed to his children as well.

Gran Gran

I didn't know that my grandmother was half white until I was an adult. I never connected her long, flowing, wavy gray hair with anything other than wanting to always brush it. It is not unusual to have a range of skin color within one black family with the same parents, as was my mother's.

My grandmother's mother, my great-grandmother, was the daughter of a slave. My grandmother's father, my great-grandfather, was a first generation German-American Jew from a very prominent family in Camden, Arkansas. He was also, for many years, Camden's County Assessor. Both of my grandmother's parents lived in Camden, Arkansas, where she was born. I have no idea of how my great-grandmother and great-grandfather got together. This coupling between white men and black women was not highly unusual in the South during slavery as well as segregation. Black women had very little, if any, control over their bodies with regard to men, including black men as well as white. This included the fact that men of either race had no obligation resulting from such unions. It should be noted that it was forbidden and assured death for a black man to even look a white woman in the eye or touch her in any way.

Adolph Felsenthal
Courtesy of Marlo B. Krueger

Daisy Felsenthal Hankins
Hankins Private Collection

I can only judge my great grandfather by his actions within the legal and cultural restraints of the times. I say this, because it is notable that he, Adolph Felsenthal, a first generation German Jewish immigrant, in the segregated

South, acknowledged paternity of my grandmother when it was the preferred custom to do otherwise. My grandmother carried her Jewish father's last name, a clear admission of paternity, which was highly unusual. She also named her firstborn son after him. It should be noted that in the segregated South it was illegal for whites and blacks to marry. It was a family rumor that he had asked my great-grandmother to move with him to Chicago, but she refused. He never married until long after her death.

Hankins Family 1954, Hankins Private Collection

My family holds Adolph Felsenthal in high esteem. Not only did he acknowledge paternity of my grandmother, he educated her in one of the most exclusive Catholic schools for black females, located in Pine Bluff, Arkansas. In commemoration of her graduation from high school he donated a stained glass window to the church of the Catholic school and convent she had attended since early childhood, which is still there. The window is there today with my grandmother's name, Daisy Anastasia Felsenthal. Biographers who chart the lineage of my great-grandfather's family say consistently that Adolph Felsenthal had no children. He did. He had one daughter, ten grandchildren and nineteen great-grandchildren. Judging from the manner in which he treated my grandmother, his daughter, he would have been proud to have known we existed.

My grandmother's connection to her father was an open secret in the town. Everyone knew who her father was. In conversation with her about it in her later years, I asked, "Why didn't you call him Daddy?" Her response, "Oh! No!" In spite of her reaction, I respect my great-grandfather for never denying his black daughter. I also remember discussing his death with my grandmother. She said that everyone was telling her that she should claim his estate. She told me that she chose not to, "Because those white people would have burned my house down by the time I got home."

I also remember as a very young girl playing patty cake with a friend while repeating a popular nursery rhyme. I thought what I was saying was, "Aca bacca, aca bacca aca abacca boo, if you mother chews tobacco, she's a dirty 'doo'." When I loudly repeated this rhyme within earshot of my mother, she spontaneously snapped at me, "Don't say that!" I stopped immediately, of course, but I didn't understand what I had done wrong, and it wasn't the right time to ask. I understood years later that what I thought was the word "doo," was really Jew. In other words, the phrase was, "Acabacca, acabacca, acabacca boo, if your mama chew tobacco, she's a dirty Jew," in other words, the song was calling someone's mother a dirty Jew. I began to wonder if my mother had been taunted as a child by other blacks because her mother's father was Jewish.

5

EDUCATION

The Black classroom – Teacher clearly in charge

The teacher's muscles from her neck to the tips of her fingers were as taut as thick fully stretched rubber bands. You could hear a pin drop as she tapped the wooden ruler with a familiar staccato snapping rhythm, slapping the palm of her hand. She sat in a chair, poised like a cobra in front of the class, jaws set, as her eyes darted from side to side, making quick visual sweeps of the classroom over her rimmed glasses, quickly making an accurate assessment of who had done their work correctly, who was unsure, and the reliable two to three students who almost never got it right. She knew everything by the look on our faces. Regardless, we knew that no matter what, we would soon find out the truth about our work.

We knew that our first grade teacher was always ready to provide lightning feedback on our work with a quick strike, like a snake bite, as punishment for the slightest hint of an infraction or lack of knowledge. She would ask you direct questions, eye to eye, when she already knew what your answers would be. You were punished with the ruler if you got a wrong answer, whether written or verbal. There were no grey areas; punishment was consistent, and everyone was treated the same. We would line up, one by one, in turn, hand our completed work for review to the seated teacher. She sat with a ruler and a red pencil in hand, correcting our work as we stood trembling nervously next to her, especially if we knew we had a wrong answer or one we were unsure of. There were only one of two outcomes from having your work reviewed: we would return immediately to our desk and either put heads down and cry, or watch the remaining group go through their individual tortured moments of suspense. We never laughed when someone cried or got the ruler; we knew if we did we would probably be next. My first grade experience was the beginning of many. It was standard discipline in a segregated classroom in the South where education was our only hope for the future. Black teachers were committed to realizing this hope, and this was the way they showed it. They held the entire class to a high standard of excellence, there were no special education classes beyond those for students with obvious mental disabilities.

Black teachers during segregation seemed to take a personal interest in their students, holding us solely accountable for our learning successes regardless of personal challenges. I remember being spoken to as though the teacher were my parent many times. I don't mean "darling" or "dearie," I'm talking about threatening, and in my face. They would ask in an "I already know what you are going to say" and a "You already know what's going to follow..." tone in front of the entire class. "And why don't we have MY homework?" or even more intimidating, "Why didn't you get MY problem right?"

My first grade teacher at Dunbar Elementary School was Miss Roundtree, a teacher who had a community-wide reputation for all of her students of being able to read exceptionally well by the time they completed the first grade.

For those of you who wish to know the details, there were three ways you could be assured of getting the ruler, usually a twelve-inch flat wooden stick with a narrow strip of metal that ran the length of the long edge. One was when you were in the lineup to get your class or homework reviewed, and you had wrong answers; you were usually given whacks on the hand, opened palm fully exposed, with bent back fingers for each wrong answer. You would walk away holding a workbook page filled with bold red "X's" and scratches to add to the humiliation and physical pain. For a higher level of infraction such as talking in class, passing notes, or chewing gum, one of the greatest infractions ever, boys were whacked on the butt with the ruler, and girls, who wore only dresses, would have the hem tightened around their legs while the teacher applied the ruler to their bare legs. There was one very creative third or fourth grade teacher, Mrs. Powell, who was notorious for throwing her shoe across the room at students if they were talking or not reading aloud well enough. Through violence and intimidation, she produced lifelong learners through no fault of their own.

Going to the principal's office for an infraction was the ultimate level of punishment, almost unheard-of. It was rumored among us students in hushed conspiratorial tones that the principal used a leather strap with holes in it that sucked out part of your flesh with each whack. I am sure this wasn't true, but I am also certain it made some students think twice before doing something that would have them sent to the principal's office and have to have the door closed. All I knew was that it was a horrible, almost unimaginable moment to be escorted to the principal's office. An immediate flood of hysterical tears was always predictable. This was reserved for boys, really bad boys, who were almost nonexistent.

Being disciplined for classroom behavior was unthinkable in my family. My parents had a zero tolerance and would admonish that "The dumbest person in the classroom can sit down and shut up!"

There may have been one or two predictable tears in the teacher's lineup, but most of us did our work, if for no other reason than to avoid the ruler. Needless to say, for us it was almost unthinkable to finish the first grade and not be able to read and write well and know basic math. If you didn't accomplish this, and few didn't, you were forever considered "dumb," and somewhat ostracized. Social pressure was too great, no one wanted to be thought of as dumb, or even have friends who were considered dumb--you had to do your best to be successful.

Like Oprah, black kids really believed that white children didn't get hit by parents or teachers. I don't recall a middle ground for punishment in school, such as demerits, diversions, warnings, or timeouts; just corporal punishment, which must have been quite effective; we never got too far out of line during segregation. In all of my six years in a segregated school I don't recall a teacher ever telling me, "Good job!" or giving me a gold star, etc. If you got all answers correct you would get a red "100%" written on your paper, but no happy face. It seems our only real positive reinforcement was the fear of the fact that we knew if we didn't learn, we couldn't do anything with our lives, and we would be destined for poverty and disgrace, to be avoided at any cost.

Taking advantage of education in order to improve your future was not an option--regardless of your situation, you had to try; there were no excuses. Teachers drummed into our heads that blacks couldn't be average; we had to be above average in order to succeed in the white world. They never mentioned the fact that whites didn't hire blacks for jobs beyond low-paying service jobs. On the whole, black teachers showed little mercy for our personal circumstances, our purpose was clear. We had to show that we were just as good as whites, preferably better. We were led to believe that an average black was considered substandard, not good enough to function in a white world. It went without saying; all students were aware that nothing was more important for blacks than getting a good education. I laugh to myself when recalling parts of some of the songs we sang at the beginning of the school day. One had the lyrics "We work together, we learn together, brothers all are we in our love for liberty...in the good old

American way!" as we sang in our substandard segregated living and learning environment. We as children had lived all of our lives within the black community where seeing whites piqued the curiosity of the entire neighborhood. Our all-black community was normal for us; we knew whites had better, but rarely had the opportunity to see the disparity in our living. It didn't matter--we were still held accountable for being and doing our best!

This was my most difficult and painful subject to write about because I have never written science fiction, and to write about black American education in the 1950s compared to our current education standards in the black community parallels a science fiction novel. It may be a stretch for most to imagine that the discipline and mental health problems as we know them today were either nonexistent, undiagnosed, or ignored. There may have been one or two in the entire school who were what was considered a discipline problem, but wouldn't be today. "Talking back" or "sassing" a teacher was unthinkable. "Bad" kids were kids who didn't always have their homework, got into fights on the playground, or didn't attend school regularly. I didn't realize it at the time, but they were also very poor as well. That's not to say that children who were poor did not perform to standard--most did, it's just that those who were considered "bad kids" were also very poor as well. In the black communities in the South, most were not considered well off, but different levels of poor. Poverty was not a legitimate excuse for not learning in a segregated black community.

Teaching a slave to read was forbidden in our past. It was a conscious way of ensuring enslavement of the mind as well as the body. While we admired our black musicians and athletes, we had a drive for education, valuing excellence beyond sports or entertainment. It is no longer popular to seek status through scholastic achievements for too many young blacks today; their heroes are reflective of this change in focus. Sadly, our greatest disappointment to ourselves and our children is that, today, unfortunately, we have created our own mental slavery. I am reminded of the words of the Negro gospel, "Oh Freedom," which we sang with great fervor at church on Sundays, which was created during Reconstruction (1865-1877) in the South after the ending of the Civil War. *"Before I'll be a slave I'll be buried in my grave and go home to my lord and be free!"* This commitment seems to have faded with our past.

School amenities

It was unthinkable for a student to show on the first day of school without adequate supplies; even if they were poor, they managed somehow. It was the parents' responsibility to provide a supply of pencils, pens, and notebooks throughout the school year, plus pay a classroom fee for art supplies and other classroom miscellany. Students took great care with their school supplies. Textbooks were assigned to us for the school year and we would often cover them with cutout brown paper sack just to preserve them to last throughout the year. It was said that black students got the books that had been used by white students, some obsolete. I don't recall this, but I also don't recall ever smelling the newness of a textbook and hearing the soft crack of a stiff hard cover against the spine that had never been opened. To black teachers it didn't matter where your books came from; you were still held accountable for learning, no excuses. Had I complained about the books, a black teacher would have probably responded, "Until you have mastered knowing everything in the book that's in front of you, you have no right to complain." No excuses.

There were no mass free lunches for poor students that we referred to as "welfare." There was a stigma attached to what I thought was termed "well fed," instead of welfare--children who received free tokens for lunch each day. Since my father was a principal at an elementary school at the time, I knew that each school was given a certain amount of tokens for poor kids' lunches. I do believe that once the tokens were gone, so was the free lunch...no food.

The school pyre in Blytheville

The sound of "Fire!" woke the labor-weary and sleepy black community in the 1920s rural town of Blytheville, Arkansas, from a rare peaceful and pride- filled sleep. My father clearly remembered how his entire community had gotten together to build their first black high school. The community was on its way up from slavery. They took the initiative and built their high school with their own money and labor. It was a community project, a source of pride for all in the black community. For one day, it made the vision of advanced education a reality for the small rural black community. Their hopes buoyed each day with the progress toward completion of what should have been a source of pride within the community--they had done it on their own.

Just as they had fallen into a well-deserved deep sleep, they were jarred awake by the smell of smoke and the sound of people yelling "Fire!" Tears, pain, frustration, and disappointment came as the glow of the flickering flames reflected in their disbelieving faces. The community learned that their efforts had been deliberately destroyed, and their ambitions for the future were wasted, burned to the ground overnight. They were back where they started, but it was worse this time; they had the reality of the frustration of trying to improve themselves when the dominant white culture clearly did not want them to. It was as though it had never happened—a light of hope in the black community that had turned to smut and smoldering ashes. The reality of the morning after was a pile of ashes attesting to the dashed hopes of what once was, and what could have been, but could never be as far as they could see. To attempt to rebuild would be in open defiance to whites, asking for trouble with the potential for worse to happen if they tried to rebuild. The ash heap would remain for quite some time.

The Ku Klux Klan were responsible for burning down the black high school the night it was completed. It would be years before members of the black Blytheville community would ever dare to attempt to rebuild it. My father managed somehow to receive his high school education and go to college against all odds. According to him, he was about ten years old before he started school in the first grade. The teacher promoted him immediately to the second grade because he knew how to spell his name.

While slavery no longer existed, segregation was representative of whites' inability to accept blacks as equals. An example of Southern whites' attitude toward black education is my father's experience as a young boy on his first job, working at a cotton gin. He was precocious at a young age. He soon became popular because he could quickly figure out how much was owed each worker before they accepted their pay. When the white overseer learned this, he quickly assigned my father to become a water boy, running back and forth to quench the thirst of the field hands picking cotton. My father was educating the field hands, keeping them from getting cheated by the white overseer who weighed and calculated their wages. This was approximately sixty-five years after the Civil War, and an example of the fact that attitudes toward blacks didn't change with the stroke of a pen.

The story must be told about the establishment of black colleges, which still exist today. They are currently open to all, and referred to as "Traditionally Black Colleges." These colleges were established during the period of Reconstruction and segregation to provide advanced education for blacks who were not permitted to attend white colleges in the South. It attests to the quality of education provided to blacks to know that such colleges produced people like Martin Luther King, Jr., George Washington Carver, Tuskegee Airmen, etc., and are still considered excellent colleges today.

Carolyn Hankins Watkins, Watkins Private Collection

The one-room schoolhouse

My earliest memories of school were when I was five years old on those rare occasions when my mother, for whatever reason, had to take me with her when she taught in a one-room schoolhouse in a small rural town outside of Little Rock called Hard Scramble. What stood out for me was a room with a huge wood stove near the front, and rows of backless wooden benches lining the classroom. I remember that "the big boys" would have to come to school early to start the fire to heat the classroom before the others arrived. This was in an extremely poor area in Arkansas. Even at my preschool age I clearly sensed the grinding poverty that these children were experiencing. My family was rich in comparison. I remember my mother always giving our old clothes to her students. There was one older girl, Marie, who must have been poorer than the others. I remember her coming to school early as she would stand in the back closet away from the potential peering eyes of the soon-to-arrive students as my mother used safety pins to arrange her clothes before class started. In spite of the level of poverty of the children of black sharecroppers in Hard Scramble, these students were held to the same standards; as with any others, poverty was no excuse for not excelling. As with most black teachers during segregation, my mother had compassion for her students' circumstances, but it was still no excuse.

6

OUR COMMUNITY – WHAT IT WAS LIKE

The Black family

I will never forget the feel of my body trembling from the overwhelming unfamiliar sounds of the drumming vibrations of pain in my head as my young eight-year-old mind made every effort to grasp the surreal, the unthinkable, to make sense of the overwhelming terror that gripped me as my small arms clung with all my strength to my father's pant leg, screaming and crying over and over, "Daddy! Please don't leave! Please don't leave me!" as he, with suitcase in hand, steadily, without interruption, made his way toward the front door.

I was the younger of two girls. This was incompre -hensible to me. I truly believed that if I begged my father from the bottom of my heart and showed him how much he meant to me, he would do as I had asked--he would not leave me. He did. Some today might say that at least I knew who my father was. The unthinkable had happened to my family; my parents separated and my father left us and moved to Colorado Springs, Colorado to get his master's degree from Colorado College. For many years, after he returned to us, he wore his Colorado College T-shirt with the roaring tiger's head until it had faded, was in tatters, and nearly fell off of him. I don't recall it ever graduating to the next level of a dust cloth, as with other old T-shirts and rags in our house. It just quietly and uneventfully disappeared. No one ever acknowledged its absence or spoke of it. In retrospect I have come to realize that the Colorado College T-shirt meant more to him than just an ordinary, white cotton college T-shirt.

For my father to leave us was an extremely rare occurrence in our circle of the black community. Not to provide excuses for his behavior, but I do recall this family trauma occurred around the time my father had applied for a job with the federal government. It must have been a significant one that he was clearly qualified for, because I remember my mother showing me a letter he had received from the governor of Arkansas, Orval Faubus, who a few years later would make every attempt to stop desegregation in Arkansas, including the Little Rock Nine. From what I remember, the governor's letter explained to my father why he, as a Negro, could not get the job for which he had applied. I was too young to understand or remember the details.

In my young mind there was no difference between being separated or divorced; the end result was the same: a father was no longer in the home. This is not to say that I wasn't aware of those who had no father in the home because "they got killed in the war." To me it was completely different because children of divorced and separated parents had fathers who chose not to be there. In those days it was even rarer for a mother to leave her family--I knew of none; mothers usually always stayed with their children.

The feelings I was left with were enduring, everlasting, regardless of the outcome. Even though my father eventually returned to our family, I had to deal with the unhealed scars of rejection, the deep feelings of humiliation, and the public embarrassment around the fact that I thought everyone knew my father no longer valued me as much as I had thought previously. Things were never the same. I am sharing this because the impact of an absent father, even one who has chosen to come and go in your life, lasts a lifetime.

Yes, I am speaking of fathers in America in general, and black men specifically, because black families with a husband-wife family are only 29% of black families with children, and white husband-wife families are 64%, according to the 2010 US Census. The devastation families suffer because of absent fathers and the devaluation of fatherhood in our society is reflective of the dramatic shift in the values that were the primary ingredients contributing to a cohesive black community.

The 1965 report "The Negro Family: The Case for National Action" by the Secretary of Labor, Daniel Patrick Moynihan, stated that "households diminished the authority of black men with their families, leaving them unable to serve as responsible fathers...." As a result, the black family unit was fragile.

After over two hundred and fifty years of slavery, segregation was the first opportunity former slaves had to begin to form strong traditional, two-parent families. Black families were recovering from hundreds of years of destabilization of family relationships. Any sense of personal family connection had been destroyed during slavery. Slaves had no legally recognized marriages. Men and women slaves lived together and had children, but the permanence of these bonds was determined at the whim of the slave master. Overnight, without warning, any and all could be sold--each family member could be sold separately to different buyers, never to be seen or heard from again, the same as they would treat livestock.

Segregation was the first time blacks in the South, where most lived, had the opportunity to begin creating strong family units. Blacks' efforts to create strong family units continued throughout the Civil Rights Movement, and then the women's movement began.

In my opinion, the destabilization of family is one of the unspoken outcomes of the Women's Movement during the '70s, which is described as the "second wave" of their movement because white women had previously won the right to vote in 1920, excluding black women. For black women, the right to vote had to include black men as well, because unlike white men, black men were as disenfranchised as black women. Black women had always been equal to their men, especially for purposes of survival with regard to work. Black women worked with their men in the fields during slavery and continued doing their share during post slavery sharecropping in order to feed their families. Even if during segregation a black woman didn't work in the fields sharecropping, she still worked by being a domestic cleaning houses for whites or as a washerwoman, working in laundries, and rarely, for the better educated, teaching and nursing.

Unlike the average white American father, whose earnings allowed him to support his entire family, including a wife who stayed at home as a housewife, black fathers usually didn't earn enough to support their families. Blacks were routinely paid less than white workers for the same task. This practice of paying blacks less was pervasive throughout America, even for black workers in the White House. Black men were particularly disparaged during segregation, and had few employment opportunities beyond labor unless well-educated. To have a two- parent family that afforded the mother to stay at home because the father earned enough money to support his family was what black people strived for. We wanted the kind of family life that white women during the Women's Movement seemed to be rejecting. Another critical aspect of the Women's Movement was that it seemed to give the subliminal message that men weren't really necessary in a family, and that women could do it all themselves. This ran counter to what blacks sought.

Black families were stabilizing under the new freedom and privileges resulting from the Civil Rights Act of 1965. I remember hearing older black women commenting about the Women's Movement being the white women's movement, and that black women would have loved to have had a husband who wanted her to stay at home because he earned enough to be the sole breadwinner. We wondered how a group of, to us, pampered white women, could consider themselves as having a Civil Rights cause, particularly one on par with the black Civil Rights Movement. We quietly said among ourselves, "I bet it is going to be easier for a white man to accept equality of a white woman, as opposed to blacks." Most black women sought the complete opposite of what white women wanted; we saw the women's movement as the white women's movement. According to the 2013 data provided by the National Kids Count Data Center, which tracks the well-being of children in the United States, 67% of black children in America live in families headed by a single parent compared to the national average of 35%. Too many black children are being raised by a single parent.

As I experienced it, the nation suddenly turned its attention to the Women's Movement and subsequently the Vietnam War, their momentum had begun. This ended the momentum of the black Civil Rights Movement.

Claud Anderson, Ed.D., in his book Dirty Little Secrets About Black History, It's Heroes, And Other Troublemakers, in my opinion, said it best:

> *Even before the ink was dry on this nation's affirmative action policy in the late 1960's, women in general, and white women in particular, had usurped blacks.*
>
> *The women's issue is a class issue and should never have been equated to that of blacks. Women are not minorities in any sense of the word. Nor have they ever been segregated, enslaved, castrated or required to be uneducated. They have always had access to this nation's socioeconomic resources through the white male. It is disingenuous to give white males a choice between assisting women or blacks. The historical role of the white male is*

protector of white womanhood. Everything in his culture drives him to share with women because as a majority, their paths will sure intertwine. White women will be his daughter, wife, mother, sister or another female within his race. ...Women were much more preferable to blacks.

Black Communities

Ninth Street

In the South, during segregation, we lived on streets with blocks; some streets were paved or gravel roads, and some had dirt roads. One difference I clearly remember is that our community in Little Rock must have been relatively compact, because I don't remember a good or bad neighborhood. Many blacks owned their own homes, and "wealthy" blacks often shared the same block as with the not-so-wealthy. You could tell where the wealthy blacks lived by the grandness of the construction of their homes, usually brick, and often two-story. One such home stands out in my childhood, the Dubissons' place on Ringo Street. They owed a funeral home, and their two-story brick house was approximately half a block from where we lived. Across the street from us was a row of run-down old wooden shacks that we called shotgun houses, where one of my best friends lived. There was a black owned mom and pop grocery store, and St. Paul's Baptist Church on the opposite corner. Other than the row of shacks across the street, most homes were well-maintained, with neat lawns. As near as I could tell, this was a typical all-black neighborhood in the South.

There was a section of town called Ninth Street, where there were thriving black businesses. Black communities had businesses that were completely self-reliant. Ninth

Street in Little Rock, Arkansas was no exception; it was a busy place and had been since the 1920s. The black-owned businesses on Ninth Street consisted of restaurants, medical offices, a movie theater, beauty and barber shops, and even a pharmacy. I remember entering an office building, climbing the wide and winding marble steps to our doctor's office, Dr. Stanley Ish, who delivered me and many other black babies in Little Rock during that time. This was also the location of the black newspaper, the *Arkansas State Press*, owned by Daisy Bates and her husband, Lucious "LC" Bates, who were the people who would later lead Little Rock's desegregation efforts. They were responsible for the forming of the historical Little Rock Nine and the integration of Central High School, the white high school in Little Rock.

There was a popular café on Ninth Street where we would gather after Sunday school and treat ourselves to the popular "Joe Louis Punch," which everyone ordered. It had an image of the "Brown Bomber," Joe Louis, in a fighter pose, looking directly at you from the bottle. To me, this bottled grape soda with his image meant it was a health drink. In other words, the more I drank, the better it was for me. I would become strong as well. I hadn't incorporated the word "health" or "healthy" into my vocabulary at the time; I just knew that it was "good" for you.

Ninth Street, as with other black communities, suffered from the ravages of white mobs' destruction with the lynching of a black man, John Carter, in 1927, who was lynched because he was accused of attacking a white woman. His body was chained to a car, dragged through the city, doused with gasoline, and burned at the entrance of Ninth Street. Furniture from black businesses was used for the fire, as well as the wooden pews from Bethel AME Church, the church I regularly attended as a child.

"The Gazette reported that...all Negro business houses and residences in the vicinity appeared deserted throughout the night." Brian Greer, *Arkansas Times*, August 4, 2000. Little

Rock's last lynching was in 1927, but the terrible memories linger, a new look at Little Rock's last episode of deadly mob justice.

Even though this occurred in 1927, people were still alive when this article was written in 2000, but were still too afraid to be interviewed by the reporter. The lynching of John Carter and the subsequent white mob on Ninth Street became a little-known secret about Arkansas history; blacks were too afraid to discuss it and whites were too embarrassed to own it.

As with many black communities with business that were self-reliant, in the interest of integrating the black community and urban renewal, the black neighborhoods were destroyed. Ninth Street no longer exists; an interstate highway was constructed to run through the heart of it, leaving very little evidence that we, independent of outside assistance, existed and thrived in our own community, like Chinatowns, Japan towns, and Mexican barrios.

The Black Wall Street – Greenwood & Pine, Tulsa, Oklahoma – June 1, 1921

For some black communities, as with the burning of my father's Blytheville, Arkansas, high school the night it was completed, thriving and appearing prosperous was to their detriment. Another example of the detrimental outcome of successful communities in the South was the black community in Tulsa, Oklahoma, where blacks were extremely successful and independent. The black community in Tulsa was referred to as the Black Wall Street during World War I. As a result of its prosperity, whites rioted and looted black homes, and the black community was completely destroyed. Innumerable blacks were lynched, beaten, or burned alive. The rallying cry was "Shoot any nigger you see!" It wasn't considered a crime in

Southern states to lynch black people. As a matter of fact, during the time of the Tulsa massacre of blacks, lynching of blacks averaged two per week throughout the South in America. The Tulsa massacre included airplanes dropping bombs, as in WWI, their most recent war, in the night as black families slept. In Alice Murphy's article (2011): "The Rise and Fall of America's Black Wall Street: The Story of African American Entrepreneurships in Tulsa, Oklahoma, 1836-1921," she states: *"When the smoke cleared every African American within the city limit had been killed, wounded, imprisoned, arrested or placed in confinement."*

The riot was supposed to have started because a black man stumbled as an elevator lurched, causing him to accidently touch a white woman, and she subsequently cried "Rape." However, the real reason for the riot may have been because whites who had just returned from World War I and had difficulty finding jobs, were poor, and felt blacks had no right to be more prosperous than they were, certainly not better. The white community's sudden and organized response reflected clear advanced preparation for the massacre. An example of their organized advance preparation for the massacre was the almost immediate bombing of the black neighborhood as if at war. The contradiction for blacks was that they had created their own businesses and thrived independent of whites while respecting the laws of segregation, and were still punished. It seems that over fifty-five years after the end of the Civil War, blacks still could not establish themselves even when they had clearly adhered to the laws of segregation by staying in their place.

Blacks eventually rebuilt the neighborhood using mostly their own funds in spite of the obstacles set against them by whites such as not being allowed to reuse old bricks from the fire in order to rebuild. The Black Wall Street had a renaissance beginning in 1922, and flourished with over 240 black businesses. Subsequently, during desegregation beginning in the 1950s, as with Little Rock's Ninth Street, an Urban Renewal program (Model Cities) destroyed the neighborhood in the name of progress. And, like Ninth Street, the area was cleared for construction of highways I-244 and US 75, which ran through what was once the heart of the black community. By 1978, only two businesses remained in the Black Wall Street.

To quote from *Batesline Tulsa Straight Ahead*, Michael Bates, "The 1921 Tulsa Race Riot and the 90 years that followed," May 30, 2011, "Years later, Jobie Holderness reflected on the spiritual damage done by Urban Renewal: *'Urban Renewal not only took away our property, but something else more important- - our black unity, our pride, our sense of achievement and history. We need to regain that. Our youth missed that and that is why they are lost today, that is why they are in 'limbo' now."*

Rosewood Massacre, January 1, 1923

Rosewood, Florida was a predominantly black community that was self-sufficient. By 1920, the community of over 300 residents supported a school, churches, a turpentine and sugar cane mill, as well as general stores. A Rosewood survivor, Robie Mortin, described the community, *"Rosewood was a town where everyone's house was painted. There were roses everywhere you walked. Lovely."*

As with the Black Wall Street Massacre in Tulsa, Oklahoma and the lynching of a black man in Little Rock, Arkansas, a woman accused a black man of rape. Over 200 men from the neighboring white communities burned the town of Rosewood to the ground, including slaughtering of their animals. The white men searched the black community for the accused and suspected accomplices, and found the alleged accomplices without finding the accused. One of the accomplices was captured and jailed; the other was lynched. Many of the residents hid in swamps to survive for several days before being rescued. It is said that only the women and children were rescued because the rescuers feared mob reprisal if they rescued a black man. The former residents of Rosewood left, never to return, and the town ceased to exist. One house and the white-owned general store were what remained. Today, there is only a historic marker designating the area as a Florida Heritage Landmark.

Ocoee massacre, 1920

On the day of the 1920 presidential election in Ocoee, Florida, a riot ensued because a black man who had previously been denied the right to vote returned with a gun in order to ensure his right to vote. Blacks were registered to vote, but the local Ku Klux Klan warned, "Not a single Negro would be permitted vote." The riot resulted in the killing of approximately 500 blacks; the rest were driven out of town, never to return. Like Rosewood, blacks had to leave their homes and everything they owned to flee into neighboring communities. As a result, Ocoee became an all-white town.

Walter White, a Civil Rights activist who led the NAACP, and appeared to be white, visited the neighborhood shortly after the riot as he mingled with the local whites. "*The massacre may have been precipitated by the white community's jealously of the prosperous African American landowners.*"

The segregated Black communities – Urban Renewal

In spite of the fact that blacks were restricted to black communities and were adhering to segregation laws by staying in their places, the unspoken message to blacks, in my opinion, was that in order to be tolerated by whites, they had to keep a low profile and be subservient, and never have a lifestyle that was equal to or better than whites. This was in spite of the fact that the black community was supported and sustained by black people, completely independent of whites. Many black communities had their own professionally trained doctors and lawyers. We had our own grocery stores, drug stores, newspapers, beauty and barber shops, movie theaters, libraries, funeral homes, churches, and our own segregated elementary and high schools taught with qualified black teachers. Urban Renewal in the 1950s through the 1970s, regardless of its intentions to better communities, resulted in the destruction and displacement of many black as well as other minority neighborhoods. According to Sarah William's article, *Urban Renewal - Eminent Domain Progress in the Making: A Closer Look*":

"The obliteration of businesses, the repositioning of people, and the use of eminent domain as an officially authorized instrument to repossess private property for city-initiated projects. In the 1960s, James Baldwin famously renamed Urban renewal, 'Negro Removal.'

African American neighborhoods were destroyed for the sake of building new businesses and better roads, public housing, designed for transitional living, was bombarded with people looking for a place to live, becoming permanent, multi-generational living for many families."

My father told me that throughout his childhood, his grandfather, who reared him and owned a barber shop in their all- black segregated community, would frequently admonish him, "Never work for the white man! Don't depend on him for anything!"

The black community was a good example of "It takes a village...." If as a child you were to attempt some form of malfeasance, you not only had to hide it from your parents, but your neighbors as well. Everybody was always watching out for you. It was not unusual for a neighbor, usually a woman, to stick her head out of her window and chide a group of children for some observed misbehavior. The usual response was a corrected behavior with an automatic, "Yes, ma'am..." with fervent hopes she wouldn't report what she had just seen you do to your parents, which she usually did. Neighbors felt responsible for not letting children get too far out of line. Not that we were angels, but great emphasis was placed on the fact that what we did in public, particularly with regard to children's' accepted behavior standards, was not only reflective of the child, but their parents as well. We knew that we were really in trouble when we displayed behaviors that would embarrass our parents. Children's behaviors were reflective of their parents' ability to teach them "good home training." It went without saying that all adults were treated with respect and always referred to with the prefix of "Sir" or "Ma'am." It was considered highly disrespectful to call any adult by their first name alone; you had to preface it with Miss, Mrs., or Mr., always. The prefix of "Ms.," was not used until the second wave of the Women's Movement, which was after the Civil Rights Movement.

The minority communities of today, while consisting mainly of blacks and other minorities, bear very little resemblance to the all-black communities in the South during segregation. Unlike other ethnic communities which have existed and are still established, it's as though thriving black communities never existed. Unfortunately, through well-meaning efforts of the '50s through the '70s, we are left with slums and inner city projects that became that way, not because the residents were black, but because the inner city housing was either substandard, or lacked provisions for regular maintenance such as garbage collection. Unfortunately, those who don't know our history in America look upon the inner-city slums as a place where blacks have always lived.

Black Churches

The calm, fragile-appearing old black grandma-looking lady wore a starched white cap perched at a jaunty angle secured with hairpins on top of her fuzzy grey hair. She sat calmly with hands folded quietly in the lap of an equally starched stiff white dress. Things were quiet throughout the service until the minister approached the podium. Without warning, all of the little old ladies in white became the minister's cheerleaders. Instead of pom-poms, the ladies had their canes, crutches, or walkers that they flung full force with outstretched arms piercing the air, screaming repeatedly, "Thank you Jesus! Thank you Jesus!" As I sat next to one I quietly cursed under my breath and temporarily made a solemn vow to never be late for church again.

I lived in fear of the "shouter's row"--that's what I called it. The shouter's row was the front pew of the church, where, I believed, only highly religious people sat, and late arrivals like me who stood out for everyone to see because we would be the only ones on the bench who were not dressed in the starched white uniforms from head to toe. It was unfortunate that I fell into the latter category, because any spiritual expectations I may have had upon arrival were quickly dashed by the fear and loathing of where the usher would guide me to sit. The women of shouter's row were easily identifiable; they all sat on the front row with varying styles of gray hair topped with small pointed white caps. They wore white from head to toe--dresses, stockings, and shoes. At first glance, these swarthy visions in white gave a false sense of calm, sanctity, and serenity. I was a child; I did not understand these things. All I knew was that if I arrived late for church service at my regular church, or was late visiting a church, the ushers would invariably direct me to sit on the front pew dominated by the staunch members of the shouter's row. Avoiding the row was one of my greatest motivators for being on time for a Sunday service.

The unabashed expression of their feelings went on steroids as soon as the minister hit a phrase that resonated in some way. A few select on the row would start a personal conversation with God out loud, as the minister preached. One of the women would yell, "Make it plain!" Another would say loudly, "My Lord!" another would loudly proclaim, "Preach!" as she would raise her cane high in the air and continue to do so at regular intervals throughout the sermon. This was just the beginning, and I would have asked for being in the middle of all of this by being late. All because I was standing in front of the mirror too long, getting the curl to hang right or the seam in my stocking straight. Was it worth it?

As the sermon wound down with the preacher having repeatedly yelled and pleaded his message, the shouter's row would begin in earnest. It didn't matter what they held in their hands; when they started shouting, everything seemed to be fair game, or so I felt as a child.

I was terrified when ladies on shouter's row would flail their arms in the air, fainting, screaming, crying, jumping up and down, and even sometimes running up and down aisles from the front to the back of the church, and then back again, all the while being facilitated by a calm usher or ushers, depending on the severity, fanning or holding a box of tissues, sometimes both. It could be counted on that one of the women would stiffen and lose control, and would have to be carried out of the church by several ushers, in a horizontal position. I would cringe knowing that at any moment one of these women would either hit me, or start shouting uncontrollably and do who knows what to me. When all of these things happened at once it was considered a good sermon--the preacher really preached. The last passing of the collection plate usually brought a sense of calm on the row. My fear and anxieties over being placed on the shouter's row lasted until my late teens. I was never harmed, but, like the adage about a coward, I died a thousand deaths whenever I was late for church.

The black church in the black community, regardless of denomination, with the exception of the Catholic Church, was a sight to behold for the uninitiated. One's first impression would be that black people speak to God in very familiar tones, truly believing He heard their every word. One modern philosopher referred to the definition of the word "real" as being on the level of black people's unflinching belief in God, that He is as real as you or I. It would be an understatement to say that on the whole, black people consider themselves as having a personal relationship with Him. The second impression would be the degree of fervor, and unabashed outpouring of expression that underwrote those feelings. This was the general atmosphere in most black churches, even for many today.

A black minister held his congregation in the palm of his hand each Sunday, and for the more influential, it extended throughout the community on a daily basis. But regardless, every black minister was charged with being able to quake the soul of his congregation each Sunday. If he couldn't, he wouldn't last long. He had the responsibility of not just delivering a message; it had to be given with great drama, enunciation, voice inflections heretofore unheard of, reaching a feverish pitch that brought a profusion of sweat on his face and a flood of tears from his congregation. Your soul felt cleansed until the next Sunday.

I was raised in the African Methodist Episcopal Church, commonly referred to as AME. It is a Protestant denomination that is steeped in African- American history. It was founded in Philadelphia in 1794 by Richard Allen, a black man who, while permitted to attend a white church, was asked to leave when he went to the altar to pray. Like Catholic churches, when compared to other black denominations, the AME church is considered quite formal and ritualistic. They have a shouter's row, but mostly the rest of the congregation does not participate, unlike other black denominations. They had good choirs, but were more restrained than other dominant black denominations in the South.

Blacks in the South during segregation were either Baptist, Methodist, Catholic, or something that we children referred to as a Sanctified Church, which was really apostolic. The Sanctified Church was the most interesting to us, because they seemed to do nothing but dance and sing from morning to night, all with the sound of a loud piano, drums, and tambourines, and maybe a guitar. This was quite a contrast to my solemn AME upbringing. My grandmother in Camden, Arkansas, owned property that was rented to what we called a Sanctified Church. I clearly remember hearing church services, singing and playing of drums from early morning to nightfall.

Church was an important part of one's social status. When meeting someone new, after establishing who their "people" were, the next question would be to ask which church they belonged to. It seemed that almost everyone attended church on Sunday--they just did. Church, especially Sunday service, was an integral part of the segregated community. As with the church's role during slavery, it provided spiritual, social, and emotional support. Looking back, this was the only consistent, positive and supportive experience for the black community.

I know of many who would dance and party late Saturday night, but would always manage to rise to the occasion and attend church on Sunday. It allowed for a weekly soul cleansing, a chance to start over at the beginning of the week. The black church fulfilled a basic need to feel uplifted and supported by people with shared experiences of being treated as inferior. They also shared with passion, common beliefs in a higher power who understood, and would "see them through." The black church and its ministers played an integral role in black survival in a segregated black community, and during slavery as well.

Black ministers usually took leadership in forming attitudes and opinions with regard to social and political issues as well as basic religious beliefs. A famous example is Martin Luther King, Jr., and the many black ministers who came together to form Civil Rights Movement. During times of segregation, especially during the era in which blacks fought for Civil Rights, black churches played an integral role. They became the meeting places for galvanizing groups within the community, and to articulate the black voice nationally. In my opinion, much of the success of the Civil Rights Movement was a result of the commitment of the black ministers and their ability to motivate their communities for the cause. Black churches were quite influential in the community; it seemed that everyone belonged to a church, which was an integral part of the segregated community. They were considered by many to be the most powerful and influential black institution in the South. Without their influence and mastery of community organization experience, I believe that it would have taken longer for the full implementation of the Civil Rights Movement. The black church served as the hub of the Civil Rights Movement.

Times have changed, and while we are grateful for our past, we must exercise our individual freedom through the use of critical and independent thinking, and we can speak for ourselves, and act on our own. Black people, as with other minorities, no longer need a leader or spokesperson to represent us as one thought. We have varying opinions and values, as with any other group.

There has been very little change in America's religious institutions since segregation. Martin Luther King described Sunday mornings as the most segregated hours in America, and it's still mostly true in America today. One need only drive by as congregations are dismissed from services to see this. There are some religions that have more integrated congregations, but to this day there are many whites who attend all-white churches, and blacks who attend all-black churches. The American tradition of separate churches seems to be apparent in new cultures in America as well; however, many require services in languages other than English to accommodate their congregation's needs.

Restaurants

The Lido Inn

I wasn't aware of it at the time, but sometimes I was used as a decoy to enable the violation of one of the South's most sacred rules, "race mixing," and the worst ever, a black man and a white woman together. I was, at the age of five, an unwitting participant in one of the most dangerous acts that could be committed in the South, a black man with a white woman driving almost alone, at night, and I was their safety net. If this had ever been discovered I am sure my uncle would have been beaten, or worse, killed. I know of no other black man in the South who has gotten away with anything like this and lived to tell it.

Lido Inn, Postcard

There were special evenings when one of my Aunt Lucille's best friends from work at the Lido Inn, a white woman, Martha, would visit my aunt's home in the evening after work. It would be late in the pitch black of night that I would find myself drowsy, sitting next to my uncle in the front seat. I was barely able to peek over the dashboard as I watched the headlight lit grainy beige road speed by, half listening to the adult conversation, completely unaware of the significance of the moment. The vague black and mysterious shadow sitting alone in a corner of the back seat was Martha.

The Lido Inn, where my Aunt Lucille and Martha worked as waitresses, was one of Little Rock's most exclusive restaurants. It was an enigma during segregation because even though the restaurant catered to a white-only clientele, the wait staff was fully integrated. I never knew why; no one spoke of it nor questioned it. One of my early memories is of riding with my Uncle Walter to pick up my aunt after work and seeing all of the waitresses, both black and white, laughing and talking together. They were always complaining about their sore feet.

I always looked forward to Martha's visits because they assured good times with music, whiskey, and food, even though I slept through most of it. I liked it because the house was always filled with lots of raucous laughter when Martha was around, especially when she drank too much, which she usually did. As was customary in the South, my aunt's habit was to make a pan of cornbread each day for the evening meal. Martha loved my aunt's cornbread. One of my memories is of her sitting in my aunt's living room, laughing and talking, with a huge cornbread and cold bologna sandwich. She would take huge bites from it as she chased it with sips from her bourbon-filled highball glass. The sandwich, unique to Martha's taste, consisted of a thick wad of hand-cut cold bologna stuffed inside a wedge of fresh warm cornbread, and mayonnaise. The ever- present and cheap Old Crow bourbon highball with ice that tinkled over the laughter, cigarettes and jazz, and a bologna sandwich were what summed up a visit from Martha.

The realities of segregation and who we were hit hard late at night when it was time to take Martha home. It was my uncle's duty to drive her. My job was to sit in the front seat next to my uncle while Martha sat in the back in a dark corner so that no one would know she was in the car, and even if they did know a person was there, they wouldn't be able to tell she was white. She sat so that she barely registered as a dark outline of a profile on black. Besides, who would pay much attention to a man who was obviously taking his little girl somewhere?

One can only imagine what would have happened if we had been stopped by the police--a colored man who had been drinking, with a child in the front seat and a white woman who had her fill of alcohol, if not more, hiding in one of the corners of the back seat. Needless to say, seat belts had yet to be invented.

Fisher's Barbeque

Mountains of well- gnawed and sucked barbequed pork rib bones stacked high on red-sauce-smeared paper plates, half-empty glasses, mostly with melted ginger-colored ice, with place settings marked by overflowing ashtrays. These are my fond memories of the aftermath of an at home feast with Fisher's barbeque.

Whenever we had special guest or someone from out of town, it didn't matter that my mother was considered a great cook, the first thing anyone wanted was Fisher's barbeque. My mother could demonstrate her culinary skills later; Fisher's barbeque came first.

We kids would watch quietly with eager anticipation as my mother would ceremoniously ease the huge oval-shaped white paper plates stacked high with red sauce dripping ribs covered in wax paper, from the grease-stained brown paper bags. The aroma always tantalizingly preceded this eagerly anticipated ritual as soon as the bag, held high, crossed the threshold of the front door. When the feast ended, and I had eaten my fill, I would go to sleep with the sound of adults still talking and sucking the bones clean long after the meat had disappeared.

Fisher's Barbeque was a very popular black-owned restaurant in the black community. It was obviously the best barbeque in Little Rock because it had a tremendous white as well as black clientele. Always mindful of the rituals required of the laws of segregation, the black-owned restaurant had a designated "white only" section to accommodate whites. I guess people were more concerned with getting their good barbeque orders filled than sorting out the rules of segregation.

The Charmaine Hotel

The ultimate dining experience for blacks in Little Rock, Arkansas, was the Charmaine Hotel. A heavily starched, stark white, tablecloth supporting a plate of delicious crispy fried shrimp are all of the memories I am left with. I can recall going there only once, but the essence of dignified black waiters quietly moving about in their starched black and whites remains with me to this day.

The Charmaine Hotel was named after the owner's daughter. It served as a refuge with the best of accommodations for traveling black entertainers and other distinguished blacks who traveled in the South. I am sure it was part of the accommodations and venues for famous blacks and black entertainers, what was known among blacks as the "Chittlin' Circuit." The Chittlin' Circuit consisted of theaters, clubs, restaurants, including safe routes for blacks to travel and find accommodations, not only in the South, but the East and Midwest as well. These included routes blacks could take where they were assured of finding accommodations and services that welcomed blacks, and they were safe being there.

There was The Negro Motorist Greenbook, or The Negro Travels Greenbook, which provided a listing of services, including lodgings and restaurants, that were safe and welcoming to blacks. This was a service for blacks throughout the United States. If a black person found themselves in a city without blacks, they usually made every effort to leave before dark, and were encouraged to do so by many of the locals. It should be understood that just because an area didn't have written segregation laws as in the South, it did not mean they welcomed blacks, and black people knew this. Once out of the black community, blacks were on guard and did their best to stay out of white communities where they would stand out as different and risk being harassed at best and beaten or lynched at worst.

Charmaine Hotel, June 1961, Persistence of the Spirit Collection, PS14-02, Arkansas History Commission

I recall one summer at the age of seven when I visited my aunt and uncle in Tulsa, Oklahoma. My sister and I went for a walk and got lost. We found ourselves in an all-white neighborhood and noted a group of white boys gathering rocks to throw at "those nigger gals...." We ran and survived.

Hotels and restaurants in the South, unless owned by blacks, were generally not available to blacks. I am sure that a hotel as grand as the Charmaine Hotel was a welcome oasis in the very restrictive desert of segregation.

Restaurant Etiquette

Most restaurants in the South were not available to blacks. Unless a restaurant was built in the black community, we knew automatically that it wasn't for us. With the exception of a black restaurant in the black community, a black person could not enter a restaurant through the front door for any reason. It goes without saying that a black person could not go in, sit down, and expect service; to do so invited an openly hostile and a potentially physically violent reaction. We were guaranteed of being thrown out, literally, as soon as we walked up the sidewalk toward the front door, no matter the reason. Suspicion and open hostility arose as soon as we were noted going where we didn't belong.

At best, if a black person wanted a meal from a white restaurant they would have to go to the back door and knock, and humbly ask if they could place their order, obviously to go. They would wait outside for their order to be handed to them, all without having set foot inside. Black athletes who were with integrated teams of the North and whose travel occasionally included the South usually had to wait on the bus for the white teammates to order their food while they went in, sat, and were allowed to eat. The white restaurant may have had black dishwashers and cooks, but we all knew our places.

Restaurants and public eating places, including lunch counters, were one of the places white Southerners took a stand when fighting to defend racial segregation. Their stated logic was that they should have a choice as to who sat next to them at their table. Even after integration, there were some exclusive restaurants whose practice was to break the plates that blacks had eaten from at their table. This was done in the open after they had finished eating, in front of them. This practice assured their white clientele they were not eating from the same plates, and sent a strong message discouraging any future black clientele. Civil Rights Laws had been passed that made it unlawful to refuse services in public restaurants as well as other public accommodations, but the stroke of a pen does not change attitudes.

There were "Five and Dime" stores, or Variety Stores, similar to today's Walgreens or Rite Aid, which had what was referred to as lunch counters. They were as close as we had to a fast food chain restaurant at that time. One could grab a bite to eat--a sandwich, hamburger, cup of coffee, sundae, etc.--while downtown shopping, if you were white. Blacks were permitted to shop in stores downtown, but the lunch counters were off limits. Blacks, joined by some whites, protested the lunch counter arrangement. They banded together and held what was called a "sit-in" whereby they would, as a group, occupy lunch counter seats and demand that they be served. Whites felt so strongly about blacks eating at public lunch counters that they retaliated in anger, yelling obscenities, dousing them with ketchup, coffee, sugar, whatever they could and sometimes pulling them from their counter seats and beating them, all under the watchful eyes of the local police. The Civil Rights activists were mostly college students, practicing nonviolence, and made no effort to retaliate. They made every effort to sit calmly and place their ignored orders from the lunch counter stool. The practice of nonviolence was a basic tenet of the Civil Rights Movement. The practice of nonviolence was a philosophy Dr. Martin Luther King, Jr., adopted from Mahatma Gandhi, leader of the Indian Independence Movement (1930-1931), which resulted in the downfall of the British Empire in India. Dr. King made nonviolence the practice of the Civil Rights Movement. The local police never made attempts to stop the abuse.

All of these things occurred before the existence of the ubiquitous fast food restaurants like McDonalds, Burger King, or Wendy's. I wonder how current fast food restaurants would have managed during times of segregation. Would there have been separate areas to place and pick up orders? What about the "drive through" window--would blacks have been allowed to place an order the same as whites even though they may have preceded a white with placing their order? Would there have been separate days for blacks to place orders as was the practice with zoos and amusement parks in the South? Would there have been segregated seating, or would blacks have been allowed to enter at all, just remain in the car or order outside?

7

OUT OF PLACE

Revelations

I was hypnotized with joyous anticipation as I prepared to enjoy my secret victory of having finally tasted the cool, clear stream of running water over my curious tongue. Through what I thought of as an unguarded moment, I had seized the opportunity to satisfy a long-held curiosity. For a brief moment it just felt so right, but it all ended abruptly, almost as soon as it started. The snap of hearing my grandmother's sharp-tongued admonishment of "Girl! Get away from there!" brought it all to an end.

My grandmother was always kind and loving, especially toward her grandchildren. The only other time I can remember her speaking to us using this tone was when we were scolded for walking over the cemented over well she had in her backyard. One of the few rules my grandmother had that we knew, almost as young as when we were toddlers, was to never walk across the cemented circle, or better still, to not play near it. I knew what I had done was serious; I had to stop what I was doing immediately.

But it wasn't the rare scolding from my grandmother that made this a memorable experience, it was the shock of the revelation of the ordinariness of the taste and feel of just plain water that made this unforgettable. I had just learned that the forbidden fountain was only water. I kept turning this fact over and over in my head long after I had tasted it. It was only water. I had expected more. A lot more. The revelation that it was only water overrode my disappointment.

I must have been acutely aware of segregation between

races at an early age. By the age of five, I knew my place very well. I don't recall anyone sitting me down and telling me about my knowing my place; I just knew. I don't recall the first time I became aware of the separation between blacks and whites, it just seems that I had always known. Since this was all that I knew, I didn't have a problem with it--there was a difference between blacks and whites, and their color proved it. They were better than blacks. From somewhere in my early life the message had already been imprinted that what white people have is always better than blacks because of their color. They themselves were better; therefore, they deserved better. We also believed that most were rich--at least richer than black people, or if they seemed poor they had no excuse for it because they were white. But nothing drove the message home about one's place during segregation more prominently than the ubiquitous public water fountains.

Library of Congress, Prints and Photographs Division, Washington, DC

My older sister Carolyn and I had been sent to visit our grandmother in Camden, Arkansas, for two weeks in the summer while my aunt Lois, who usually stayed with her, took some extra college courses. It was a most unusual and memorable summer. My grandmother had vision problems and we were told we were sent to stay with her to be her two eyes. She couldn't see very well, or so we thought. But once we were settled, the "old lady" took charge. She got busy preparing meals, and we learned that you could make applesauce, and lots of it, from real apples as she stirred them for most of the day in a large Dutch oven pot. We were amazed. There were Indians, which we now call Native Americans, who went down streets in the Camden black community selling freshly caught masses of fish on lines slung on over their shoulders. I recall seeing them as neither black nor white, just that Indians were different. My grandmother bought from them what she told us was a drum fish. She laid it on the speckled metal table on the back porch as it continually thumped its long body repeatedly until she cut its head off and cut it into steaks for dinner, to our wide-eyed amazement, as we watched the entire process from beginning to eating.

I clearly remember the day that my grandmother took my sister and me downtown with her. I was about six at the time, and I definitely knew what signs meant when they were labeled "white" and "colored." Most importantly, I knew which one was designated for me to use.

We were the typical six- and seven-year-olds who took full advantage of our grandmother's seeming distraction with the white saleslady; all salesladies were white in those days. We played together freely, within the limits that black children were allowed while demonstrating good home training to whites in a white environment. We knew to act civilized, to be on our best behavior. We were probably dressed in our Sunday best, or close to it, for the trip to town. Black people usually dressed up in their best to go downtown where they were seen by whites. I am sure that we knew better than to touch the merchandise or "act a fool" on the floor, and we probably chose to play quiet pretend games as we moved about in a limited space, not running all over the place. I was always the curious one and would imagine "what would happen if," as opposed to the actual doing of anything. The stark differences between the two fountains, and the fact that I was forbidden to drink out of one, were what probably piqued my curiosity to the breaking point. The bold step of satisfying quickly my forbidden curiosity was encouraged by the shroud of assurance that my grandmother who had reared ten children was distracted and wasn't paying attention to us, which was my all clear to go signal.

The usual two separate water fountains rested against the wall in a corner across the room. The hum of the cooler from the white fountain beckoned me. The temptation was too great. Thinking no one was watching me, I darted over and took a quick sip from the white water fountain.

This was not unlike another incident that occurred at this age where I had assured myself that no one would notice as I freely dug my delighted dirty cupped fist deeply into the tantalizing ecstasy of the cold confetti colored Jell-O in the circular mold that my mother had so carefully prepared and refrigerated for a party that evening. As with taking a sip from the white water fountain, I did both with the firm conviction that no one would ever find out. Deep down I knew better, but an abundance of curiosity and the anticipation of the delight overrode everything that instinctively told me not to do it.

As soon as I took the sip from the forbidden water fountain, I heard my grandmother's immediate rebuke. I obeyed, and that was the end of it and the beginning of something else I was unable to fully understand at the time.

This brief episode was a revelation, the shock of which I have never forgotten. The white people's water in my mouth tasted no different from the colored people's water! I had fully expected white people's water to taste at least sweeter. It didn't. It was just water, except it was cooler, and in all probably it came from the same pipe.

When you see a picture of the white and colored fountains side by side, you will understand what piqued my curiosity, and tempted me in an unguarded moment one hot summer's day. It was like having a finger "accidentally" pass by a chocolate cake and getting a smear of the frosting before it is served. The white water fountains were white upright contraptions with an electrical system that hummed as it provided a stream of ice-cold water for whites. By contrast, the colored fountains were usually a small dirty bowl with a spigot attached to the wall, and no electricity to cool it. As with other provisions for blacks and whites, the white water fountain was far superior to the black one in function and appearance. It represented clearly the disparity in treatment, and what whites perceived as the inferiority of blacks, undeserving of equality.

In spite of the shock and disappointment of learning that it was just ordinary water, not something special and concocted solely for whites, I began to understand the obvious message intended for blacks was that we were not good enough to share, even touch, the same things as whites. It was just the way things were. I would learn to understand that it wasn't about the water at all; it was about living completely separate lives justified by reinforcing the convenience of the myth of racial superiority over an easily identifiable group that had been enslaved for more than two hundred and fifty years in America. At the time this demonstration of superiority through a water fountain was, to me, the greatest revelation of all. Things substandard were all blacks deserved. We survived the humiliation, segregation was the best we had, and at least it wasn't slavery.

Emmett Till

I was alone, in shock, as I sat cross-legged on the carpet of my Aunt Lucille's bedroom floor trying to turn away from what was in front of me, trying to process and to understand something, anything to give me time to comprehend the monster that suddenly appeared before me, without warning. With the casual flip of a page of the latest issue of *Jet Magazine*, my life was transformed forever. Nothing in my life had prepared me for the black and white picture of a monster in a suit, shirt, and tie, lying in an open coffin. I was eleven years old, in the fifth grade. The image kept repeating itself in my mind-- it wouldn't stop. I was beyond scared; I was terrified, my heart pounded loudly in my ears. My mind kept returning to the image, over and over. I couldn't stop the horror; it lay before me, a reality! I couldn't avoid it--the image was vivid and stayed in my mind whether I continued to look or not.

In my full view were the detailed hideous remnants of what was left of a fourteen-year-old child beaten and shot to death. What I saw was so horrible that I was stunned to the point of paralysis, unable to move even to turn the page. I was shocked to the point of feeling my brain tingle. The only thing that had come close to this experience was when I saw the movie *Samson and Delilah* (1949), starring actors Victor Mature and Hedy Lamarr. As Delilah danced the Dance of the Seven Veils, the movie quickly showed the severed head of John the Baptist on a tray with what I called at the time, "Pipes coming out of his neck!!!" But that was a movie depicting biblical times; seeing the disfigured head of Emmett Till in 1955 was a new horror, one that has never gone away. There he lay like a child's crude papier-mâché creation of a Halloween monster. He was a grotesque representation of a human being with a misshapen head almost twice the size of a normal one with something that looked like large cat gut stitching on the side of it, protruding oversized lips, and slits that exposed a grainy-seeming substance that represented eyes, a black suit, white shirt and tie, and hands that brought the revulsion to an end by having been placed serenely in a calm repose.

I had seen pictures of monsters--this was before movies were rated "Parental Discretion" or "PG-13." Movies shown in public theaters were open to all. Other movies that were not considered for public viewing were referred to as "smut" films, and were shown in places for adults only. I had always been relieved of fear knowing that monsters weren't real; at least that was what my parents had told me. I had believed what my parents told me about monsters until this moment. The image of Emmett Till was real, and he was monstrous. Not only was he real--this previously normal-looking boy had been beaten and murdered because he was a black man who didn't stay in his place. I became numb, quiet, with a feeling of the most vulnerable quiet terror when I realized that he was fourteen, only three years older than I was. The message was clear to all: *This is what they do to you when you get out of place, even children.* I got it. I had better watch out. This was the greatest racial shock of my childhood.

To my horror, I realized suddenly that my parents could not protect me if I crossed the line or got out of place. This meant that white people were above my parents and could do anything they wanted to me. This child had been taken out of his bed at night to have this done to him--his aunt and uncle could not protect him from white rage, they had no regard for them, who he was staying with for the summer. This was clear evidence to me that whites ruled over blacks. My sense of complete naked vulnerability was almost indescribable. I vowed always to stay in my place, as though my life depended on it. I felt that if I got out of place, white people could come into my house at night and take me away and kill me, and my parents could do nothing, like his aunt and uncle, but watch them, like Emmett Till.

The reality of the depths of racial brutality, the horrors of race hatred manifesting itself in a fourteen-year-old boy who got out of place jolted the black community nationwide. I cannot imagine a black person at that time who was not shaken to the core upon seeing the mutilated corpse of Emmett Till displayed publicly. His mother insisted that he have an open coffin to display the brutality for all to see, and that's what I saw as a fifth grader. It was in the fall of 1955 that you could heard black adults talk about "what they did to that colored boy from Chicago down in Mississippi!"

I have never forgotten the moment I first saw the remains of Emmett Till. The feelings have lasted a lifetime. I can close my eyes today and immediately recall every detail of this experience.

I knew about lynching. There was a family story about my Uncle Hesterly, who, as a young boy was in the woods alone and was seen by a group of white boys who cried out as soon as they saw him, "There's a nigger, let's get 'em!" Whether they were serious or not we will never know, because my uncle outran them. These were times when the lynching of blacks, especially men, was not a surprising outcome for any controversy involving whites. It was done with impunity for at least one hundred years after slavery ended in 1865. The lynching of blacks was an effective and efficient means for the imposition of white supremacy. Through fear and intimidation, it was a sure way to keep blacks in their place. Lynching brought an immediate end to any perceived misbehaviors. The impression it left on blacks was lasting. Emmett Till was not lynched, but it had the same effect. Lynching was a crime committed against blacks with impunity, yet our Congress was never able to implement an anti-lynching law even though the practice continued until the late 1960s. In spite of the brutality of the murder of Emmett Till, as with lynching, no one was ever punished; the two white men suspects were acquitted even though one admitted to the killing in a later magazine article. It was inconceivable to charge a white man for any crime against a black person. Besides, all courts and juries were white, but it never got that far anyway. The message was loud and clear to me: I must always make certain that I stayed in my place.

WATERMELON and other self-imposed restrictions

It was a routine hot summer's day when I sheepishly eyed the very generous wedges of precision-cut pyramid shapes of row upon row of bright-red, ice-cold watermelon. They were lined in neat rows like a military parade, displaying sharply cut edges on white plates in a self-service restaurant. Saliva filled my mouth as I relived countless memories of the satisfaction of a quick cold and crisp chomp that yielded an abundance of sweet juices. Enough of the fantasy, I thought, coming to my senses. I realized that I was older now, so I knew better. But I was in the presence of whites, so I ignored the watermelon and reached for a plate of cantaloupe instead.

Ignoring the watermelon, which I preferred, was an automatic reaction in public, especially around whites. This habit survived long after the Civil Rights Movement. I had felt an obligation to quell the long-held stereotypes of blacks during slavery and segregation, even though most people today probably didn't remember them. I remembered. I had been conditioned as a child to not fulfill the stereotype. I couldn't help it. My avoidance of eating watermelon in public was almost without thinking, ingrained in my subconscious. Even though I craved it, I would never give whites the satisfaction of seeing me eat it. Until recently, I hadn't realized that such a benign fruit as watermelon had such a major impact on what I ate in public for most of my adult life!

Before the Civil Rights Movement it was commonplace to

depict black people with big red lips, gapped white teeth, always smiling and eating watermelon. It was a standard and widely accepted practice to portray blacks, particularly black boys, raiding a white farmer's watermelon patch and being in such states of ecstasy that they could barely make it over the fence before sitting down and eating it. The implication of the myth was that we were childish and simple-minded, had no impulse control, and we would steal anything, especially watermelon. We couldn't help it, we found watermelon irresistible. It was graphics like "Currier & Ives," which was a very popular illustrator of American life that was regularly published in the widely distributed *Harper's Magazine* that perpetuated the myth that all black people wanted to do was to be happy eating watermelon...at any cost, including stealing and risking their lives at the point of the white farmer's shotgun! We were depicted eating watermelon and spitting seeds as though it was the greatest thing that had happened to us. Currier & Ives, popular 19[th-] and early 20[th-] century illustrators of American life dedicated an entire series of their illustrations to "Downtown Darkies," specifically aimed at denigration of blacks, of which the watermelon depictions were a part. It bears mentioning that for the most part, blacks were usually portrayed as happy and carefree, as they were during slavery, no matter the age or circumstances. These portrayals of blacks were once quite ubiquitous in American culture.

Seeing the depiction of blacks in both illustrations and movies made me extremely self-conscious about eating watermelon in public places, including picnics. It symbolized to me the fulfilling of white people's negative perception of black people. I certainly didn't want to be grouped with the image of the buffoonery of blacks over watermelon as they were portrayed; I felt that to eat watermelon fulfilled the myth. If given the opportunity to choose between honeydew, cantaloupe, and watermelon –

my choices were honeydew, cantaloupe or even a papaya or a mango, but NEVER watermelon! I guess that somewhere in my forties or fifties, it just went away, and one day, without my realizing, it was gone!

Watermelon, Postcard

It had taken me literally decades of my adult life before I could comfortably eat watermelon in a public place. I guess one of the things that made it okay was when I noticed that not only black people enjoyed watermelon, white people did as well. I noticed that cultures other than black or white seemed to enjoy it as I did, especially Asian and Hispanic cultures. The good news is that today I can sit on a beach, picnic bench, or fine restaurant at high noon, and unselfconsciously eat the entire contents of a watermelon with my bare hands! It bears mentioning that things don't change because of the stroke of a pen.

Black people steal

The store manager stood a few feet away from me, eyeing me suspiciously between his fake attempts to straighten magazines, as I searched the rack of sunglasses deciding on the best pair to buy. I guessed that I was taking too long. He was now idly thumbing through the magazines, pretending to read them, frequently peeping over the top to steal quick glances toward me as in some comedic spy movie. The only difference was that this was not a movie--the store manager was dead serious and this was real. He stayed in the magazine rack for an inordinate amount of time and then began arranging and rearranging the crackly cellophane bags of popcorn, which were nearer to me. It was painfully obvious to me that I was being watched. I was not shocked; this was all too familiar. I made my purchase and left the store as the manager moved away to do other things.

Even today, I cannot walk into a store--any store, from a simple corner drug store to a high-end department store--without feeling that I am under suspicion, always being watched solely because I am black. I make it a point to keep everything that I touch in the open, so that I am not suspected of stealing. I keep my hands visible at all times. This isn't a chore; I have been doing this all my life, and I do it almost without thinking. Long ago I learned as a child that whites felt that blacks could not be trusted, and that our second nature was to steal things. I have not been able to let this one go, because it seems to be reinforced by store managers, sales, and security, at any store I visit, even in my current daily life.

EPILOGUE

My first real education

My cheeks stung from embarrassment about something I could do nothing about. I had something that I could not change that was out there for all to see, I could not hide it. I kept chiding myself over and over--how could I have been so stupid, forgetting my blackness, letting my guard down and forgetting my place for one moment?

It was the last day of school of my first year in an integrated school that ended my temporary delusion as to who and where I was. A group of white girls in my home economics class at my new school in Los Angeles, Horace Mann Junior High School, took care to remind me. I had my first direct experience with "in your face racism," not in the segregated South, but in an integrated school in California. Within three months of graduating from the sixth grade, after six years of segregated education, my family moved from my all-black community in Little Rock to enroll me in a predominantly white, primarily Jewish junior high school, in Los Angeles, California. I was completing my first year in an integrated school.

That first year taught me that it was not just the South where racism was practiced, but in most of America. In the South it was made clear where a black person's place was, but in what we thought of as an integrated California was made more difficult because there were no laws that defined a black person's place. One had to either anticipate racism and to always be prepared before one arrived in a new area, or bounce against walls like a blind person with no cane until they became familiar with the unspoken boundaries of their designated place. We use to say that at least in the South you clearly knew who the enemy was, but this was by far not true for other places in America.

My parents had bought a home in Los Angeles that was in a neighborhood in transition from all white to black. The neighborhood school was still predominantly reflective of the white population in the area. I was the only black in my all-girl home economics class. The separation of the sexes was deliberate; boys took "shop" classes instead. What shop consisted of I will never know; all I remember is that it was quite noisy. I had developed what I thought was a classroom friendship with the other girls at my work table--at least they seemed cordial and open to me. They must have gotten used to my presence and openly discussed what to do with our class project at the end of the semester. The class assignment for the semester had been to complete a skirt, blouse, and an apron. All I remember is that our talk evolved into a plan for a group of us girls deciding to wear our outfits on the last day of school. That decision logically followed to meet afterward at the nearest café for hamburgers and malts. I was excited--I was included in the group planning, everything, but in retrospect I don't think they took me seriously, and certainly didn't mean to include me. I was just there, and felt included because of the open discussion around me. I was excited. My mother gave me extra money for the after-school date with the girls.

I arrived to class on the last day, outfitted and excited, and wanting to talk about it as girls do. I was met with an awkward silence. They all sat around the work table looking away from me, avoiding eye contact. Each girl, one by one, never gave a reason beyond "My parents said I can't go!" I sat in silence for the rest of the class, cheeks burning, waiting for it to end. I learned later that a parent took the group of girls to the café in their outfits after school that day.

I couldn't wait for school to end. As I was licking my wounds and trying to be invisible, or at least do the impossible and hide my blackness, a white girl who wasn't in the class, but one who had befriended me that year, came up to me and said, "I want you to go with me after school to have a hamburger and a malt!" Her name was Darlene Lattman; all I knew was that she had told me she was something called a Christian Scientist, whatever that meant. I declined her invitation because the day had been too much for me. She persisted, and I knew that she meant it, but all I wanted to do was to end the school year and just go home and lick my wounds. That was over sixty years ago--I never forgot it. I hope that Darlene has lived long enough to read this and know that her kindness was very much appreciated, and remembered for all of these years.

Horace Mann Junior High School

For my parents it was extremely important that my sister and I attend the best schools they could afford, which translated into the nearby previously all-white neighborhood public school, Horace Mann Junior High School. The neighborhood we lived in was in the beginning stages of a major transition, because there were approximately thirty black students, and about five Mexicans in the entire school. I don't recall there being any Asian students. There was one black teacher, Mr. Childs, and two Asians, Mr. Hashibara and Mrs. Zasada, who were Japanese. Blacks, being the majority of minority students, and easily identifiable, were the embarrassment of the school because we would sit together on the bleachers at lunch time, and the Mexicans would join us. There were a few whites who seemed to be in awe of us and would join us as well. I guess they were the pre-Hippies; we all had fun being together. Mr. Childs would chide us for always congregating on the bleachers at noon each day, but we ignored him, we never stopped. The faculty must have pressured him, as the only black teacher, to speak to us about making such a separatist spectacle of ourselves. In retrospect, I am sure we were an embarrassment to the school for anyone visiting the campus and seeing the entire minority student body huddled in one place, on a row of bleachers, in the middle of the campus. It must have proven quite the sight for the previously all-white school. I believe that the white faculty were cautious about approaching a mass of black students, and due to the political atmosphere of the Civil Rights Movement, may have seen us as potential powder kegs ready to explode. They were afraid; this was new, and they were seeing masses of blacks marching in protest on TV. We may have been their first direct experience with black people. As in the South, most neighborhoods in California were segregated, but this time, instead of enforcing laws of segregation, it was done by an unwritten law. This was probably their first experience with blacks other than passing on the street.

Black people were addressing the need for change in America's mistreatment and the injustices. We were tired and angry. This must have been quite an intimidating experience for whites. They were taking a forced cold shower of immersion into an unavoidable new society. I believe that this contributed greatly to later attitudes and assumptions about black students and what were then their perceived behaviors, which have subsequently manifested into reality. Remember, heretofore, black students from the South were unquestionably respectful toward teachers. Something happened. White teachers, who were the majority of teachers in Los Angeles, appeared intimidated and afraid of black students. They weren't used to being around blacks, particularly black boys. Black students had an equal adjustment. Many had to adjust to the white teacher's way of teaching. Black students from the South were used to teachers taking a personal interest and holding them accountable for their learning. This was, in my opinion, an important element missing for blacks in integrated schools and responsible for the subsequent placement of black boys in special education classes.

We black students were always together because we lived together in the same segregated California neighborhoods where all of our family and friends were. We shared the same cold shower of having left segregation to realizing that we had moved to a new form of discrimination. While white students weren't openly hostile toward blacks, few were inclusive. Black students were pretty much all we had. On the other hand, if I were white, and seeing my environment change suddenly, and done by people who were previously subservient and now had youth who weren't, it would have required some getting used to as well. Horace Mann Junior was just reflective of the times.

Education in an integrated school

I felt like slamming the door and screaming and cursing until my mouth became dry and I could no longer speak. Unfortunately, my old automatic good behavior and my good home training took over. I left the room as rapidly as I could, but closed the door softly. I wanted to become invisible. I felt that this was the best one could do who felt embarrassed by their incredible stupidity, feeling like a fool for thinking they were good enough, certainly not as good as. Mrs. Shutt, my guidance counselor at Horace Mann Jr. High School, had just taken great pains to call me into her office to tell me in no uncertain terms that I wasn't good enough for anything beyond a service or clerical career. I was hurt deeply; my life no longer held the future I had taken for granted. She was an older buxom blonde woman who always had lots of black hair pins stuck in her vast field of black netted yellow ringlets held tightly over the front of her head. She also had bright red lips that formed two arches near the corner of her mouth instead of near the center. She never lost her toothy smile as she gave me the news with a cheerful glad to be of help attitude.

Mrs. Shutt was my guidance counselor; she was the authority. I felt she knew these things better than me or my family. She told me cheerfully that I could not go to college. She explained to me that I could not go, not because I didn't have the skills or capability, but because I wouldn't be "happy" in college. I was incredulous! This was quite a comedown from what I had been taught in a segregated school where instructors told us we could do or be anything (within the bounds of segregation and future hopes) if we worked hard enough. Being told I wouldn't be happy was a new criterion. I had always assumed college was for me. When I told Mrs. Shutt this, she looked me in the eye, still smiling, and replied cheerfully, "Then I would suggest that you go to a business college instead."

In retrospect, she was just doing her job. It seemed as though in California's newly integrated setting, a majority of black students were funneled into service careers, regardless of capacity, I was no exception. This trend seemed to change by the time I was in high school, but not soon enough for me to have avoided wasting my first semester in my freshman year.

Greatly disappointed, completely uninterested in the subject, and my family believing Mrs. Shutt, I majored in business administration my first semester in high school. What a disaster. I was so awful in bookkeeping I that near the end of the semester, the teacher pulled me aside and told me that she would pass me with a "C" if I didn't enroll in Bookkeeping II. She continued, "But if I find out you have enrolled in Bookkeeping II, I will fail you to keep you out of the class. It was the same with shorthand; I could never get the curlicues coordinated with the sounds. My first semester in high school had been wasted because I truly believed that I was capable of being only a secretary, as with many black females who were funneled routinely into business administration courses. Hopefully, as with other naive black female students, we believed that we would become private secretaries like the role of the blonde and glamorous actress, Ann Sothern, who played the private secretary, Miss McNamara, in the '50s TV show *Private Secretary*. I don't know what the guidance counselors did with black boys; it couldn't have been much better.

It was the norm to have what was classified as men's work and women's work. Women's work was made clear to us in our business courses, and it was never made clearer to me than during my first semester in high school. I became aware that I was on the wrong career path when one of my very favorite business teachers, Mrs. Wagus, explained to us, to encourage us to become good secretaries, that when she was a secretary she would arrive to work an hour early each day to make coffee and set up the office. She would also polish the office chandelier once a week so that it always sparkled. She was well-meaning, but this was the breaking point in my secretarial career.

Years later I graduated from a Traditionally Black College, Langston University, with honors. I have had secretaries, but never worked as one. I had a ball in college; I was very happy. When I first attended Langston University I had to readjust to seeing an all-black community. When I arrived on campus I remember marveling at the fact that the school administration, including the president, were black, and so were all of the class presidents, and it was a fully accredited college. It wasn't the fact that they were black--it was because they were successful blacks who had professional careers.

Continuing My Education--Hildegard and the Jewish revenge

Whites against whites

There must have been an overwhelming number of

Jewish students at Horace Mann. I was learning firsthand about a kind of prejudice that didn't include my traditional definition of racism and bigotry, blacks vs whites, or the reverse. This was my first time learning about the holocaust and the "awful" Germans, evil Nazis and "dumb Pollacks." This was twelve years after the end of World War II; things were still unfolding. The entire school vented its feelings about Germans and World War II on one blonde, short and chubby, very Aryan-appearing girl of German descent named Hildegard. She was openly and constantly ridiculed and spoken of with disdain. She had not one friend as long as I. knew of her. She and her brother were the school's outcasts, although I don't recall her brother, who was older, being treated as badly as she was. It didn't help that it was immediately obvious by her ill-fitting, and well-worn clothes and shoes, accompanied by an unpleasant odor, that she was very poor. It seemed it was okay to say or do anything to Hildegard; she didn't count. She personified what it meant to be treated like dirt. Nothing was lower than the chubby, white-blonde, curly-haired, blue-eyed, pink fat-cheeked, pearl-skinned, white-lashed-and-eye browed Hildegard. She walked about as though she didn't care, and always spoke with arrogance and hints of sarcasm. I don't know how much she knew, because everyone considered her dumb and wrong, no matter what she said or did. Even the teachers, who, looking back on it were mostly Jewish, were only slightly better than the students in treatment of Hildegard. How she kept it together during those times I will never know.

I noticed that most of the white girls were brunettes; there were very few blondes. Coming from a culture that had clear delineations between races, it was quite new to me to see that all white people didn't consider all white people the same, or even as equals. The one thing Hildegard and I had in common was that we were both the worst violin players in my orchestra class. We were second violins, but my chair was always before hers, which is the way players are ranked. Hildegard took delight in criticizing my playing, when in fact I, and everybody else in our orchestra class knew, I was at least played better than Hildegard, if nothing else. Everybody felt they were better than she was, and I took great delight in it like all the rest. But I guess Hildegard's criticism of my playing gave her some small sense of self-worth. No matter what, I am sure she thought, she was still better than a black person. I understood this; she needed to find someone or something to make up for the daily degradation, the constant belittling, and I was fair game. I didn't like Hildegard, and mistreated her like everyone else, not because she had done anything to me, but because it was the norm. I wanted to be accepted and belong. I, like Hildegard, was completely outnumbered.

There must have been Jewish students who were holocaust survivors or refugees from World War II concentration camps, because I remember girls with accents in my PE class who would talk about how wonderful and shiny their hair looked when the Red Cross nurses in the camps made them wash it every day with a special shampoo.

Before Horace Mann I had considered all whites to be white; there were no subcategories, just white people. In my mind there was no distinction between being white and being Jewish. I remember a conversation with my best friend in Little Rock, Alice, whose mother "worked for Jews," which meant she did domestic work for them. We didn't know what it meant when we talked about them, Alice just said that "if you see one, you can tell." I left it at that, thinking that if ever I saw a Jewish person, I would know immediately. However, I found myself at Horace Mann surrounded by Jews and didn't know it; they were just white people to me. This was an unanticipated new experience for me. Horace Mann was my first time experiencing white people against white people. I knew about World War II, as much as any sixth or seventh grader, but the full knowledge of the devastation of Jews, homosexuals and Gypsies, and prisoners of war was just unfolding; it was unknown to me at the time.

My first year at Horace Mann accomplished two things: it gave me my first experience in an integrated environment, and my first experience of feeling like a minority everywhere I went. There was no phase-in, no preparation. I remember on my first day they assigned honor seniors, all white, to escort freshmen around the campus to show them where classes were, etc. The escorts were referred to as "big sister" and "big brother." The intent was to develop a friendship, someone you could call on to help you through the school maze. My big sister never acknowledged me after my "tour." I overlooked it, and, like me, the school did the best it could to mire through the uncharted territory of an onslaught of blacks students attending their school.

I had just moved from my segregated community in Little Rock where there were only black people. Everything was black, black schools, businesses, doctors, attorneys, churches, fraternities and sororities, Girl Scout and Boy Scout Troops. You did not feel like a minority unless you left the black community. In other words, the more one stayed within the black community in the South, the less one felt as a minority. That's not to say that you weren't aware of the limitations of segregation, but I just don't recall reminders like separate water fountains or bathrooms in black communities, only in areas where blacks and whites intersected, such as the downtown area. Blacks were not allowed to live throughout the city. They were allowed to live only in a section of town designated for them. We could go anywhere or use anything within our black community without restriction.

Within one year my life made a complete change, almost no comparison to the life I had experienced before.

Integration, California style--unwitting blockbusters

The morning after we moved into our newly purchased home, less than six months after we had arrived in Los Angeles, my mother stepped outside with a cheerful greeting that was completely ignored by the next-door neighbor. My mother learned quickly, as did we all, that even though our location had changed, many of the reasons for moving from the segregated South had not.

The summer of 1957 ended with our family moving into the best neighborhood in Los Angeles that we could afford and were allowed to live in. While we had naively considered racial segregation behind us, it wasn't. Los Angeles was a city that practiced a quiet segregation, which was pervasive throughout America. We were learning rapidly that while in most of America there were generally no written segregation laws outside the South and parts of the Southwest, racial discrimination was actively practiced throughout. In Los Angeles, blacks were not allowed to live beyond the intersection of Western Avenue and Adams Boulevard, no matter how rich or famous they were. It was an unspoken rule that no one sold homes nor rented to blacks outside of the area designated for us. A good landmark for the dividing line was the black-owned Watkins Hotel, whose clientele and purpose was similar to the Charmaine Hotel in Little Rock, in that they both provided lodging for prominent blacks and entertainers. Whites' reaction to blacks being out of place in Los Angeles was quite similar to whites' reaction to our being out of place in the segregated South. Nat King Cole, a very famous black singer and musician, moved to Beverly Hills during this time and the word "nigger" was burned into his lawn.

We had been optimistic about the future when we left Little Rock, but we were realizing that what we left was similar to what we now faced. Schools, buses, and most of the public services that had been segregated in the South were integrated in California, but the reality was far from it. Neighborhoods were segregated, regardless of a person's ability to pay. Segregated neighborhoods led to segregated parks, schools, and stores, because the neighborhoods were saturated with a specific racial group. In Los Angeles, California in the '50s, whites actively sought to keep others unlike them out of their neighborhoods.

In our naiveté, fleeing to California's Promised Land, as so many blacks had from the South as part of the Great Migration, we didn't know it, but we were part of the wave of the blacks that contributed to white flight from inner city residential neighborhoods. For my parents, becoming a blockbuster was not their intention; they just wanted the best they could afford for their children.

When we moved to our block of mostly homeowners, there were three white people left, consisting of two families. I use the term "families" loosely, because there were no white children or young couples, just elderly whites who had been left behind. One was the elderly couple next door, the Pauls. In the beginning they didn't acknowledge our presence. My mother, being the kind heart that she always was, would acknowledge them whenever she saw them in our adjacent back yards. Things changed for the better when they were the last white family on the block and they either got used to us, or saw we were civilized, quiet, and kept our lawn neat, and there were more of us. The wife and my mother eventually turned into neighbors who chatted over the backyard fence. The Pauls later moved--I am sure it was as quickly as they could afford.

The old crippled white woman who moved just before the Pauls lived at the far end of the block, on a corner the opposite side of the street. I guess she really needed the money because she had a small sign in her front yard garden that advertised a room for rent, "Whites Only." Of course this information was passed along through the children chain, and we would knock the sign down at every passing opportunity. I don't know if the old lady died or someone came to her rescue, but one day she was just gone.

We had no idea that we had become what was termed at the time "blockbusters." It meant that when blacks bought homes in all formerly all-white neighborhoods, they were busting the block. It usually took only one or two black families to cause whites to panic, sell their homes, and flee the neighborhood. Whites moved to the suburbs away from blacks, thereby resulting in all-white suburbs and black and other minority inner cities.

To give you some idea of the caliber of the black people on our block who couldn't move to a better neighborhood no matter who they were or how much money they made, the athlete, Wilt Chamberlain, lived on the same block, but several doors down from us. Our block was lined with tall palm trees and we would joke that he was almost as tall as the trees. He drove a purple Cadillac convertible. He never acknowledged our presence; we were just a gaggle of giggling teen girls who would boast that we lived down the street from, "Wilt the Stilt," which was his popular basketball moniker. He didn't live in the neighborhood for very long, less than a year, but we were still excited and pointed out his house with pride at every opportunity. Even today, I can point out Wilt Chamberlain's house.

How it all got started

It was the summer of 1957, the year I graduated the sixth grade when I overheard what seemed at the time an insignificant phone call, my mother telling her friend that "Daisy Bates was calling around to find some students...". It was also the same summer that my parents made the decision to move from Arkansas to California. I thought we were moving to do better, go where there were more opportunities for blacks, where there was no segregation. I knew about Emmett Till and Rosa Parks and the Atlanta Bus

Boycott, but protesting segregation close to home was not in my consciousness. That made the soon to unfold major events even more jarring for me.

In Little Rock we lived a very short walking distance from Central High School, the white high school, as we referred to it. I hadn't tied the short distance from our house to the epicenter of one of America's greatest defining historic Civil Rights events until I started writing this book. My parents never said this, but I believe a major part of their decision to move to California was to the get out of Little Rock as quickly as possible because they could sense the coming reality of racial unrest in the fall. I can only imagine what it would have been like to live so close to a school where whites so openly demonstrated their hatred of blacks "out of place," on nine children. Most of the daily angry white mob would have had to go near, if not through, my neighborhood to get to Central High School.

My father went ahead to California to secure a job and housing. My mother, older sister, and I arrived later by train. My father had gotten a job working for the post office on the night shift. He had completed all of his course work for a master's degree from Colorado College, but we didn't care that he could only get a job working at night for the post office, because he at least had a job.

My last memory of Arkansas was sitting in the train station saying goodbye to my favorite aunt, my Aunt Lucille. I overheard her and my mother joking about the fact that they didn't have to sit in the colored section if they didn't want to because of the "Interstate Commerce Act," even though that's where they had chosen to sit. I didn't have a clue about what this meant; I was just overcome with sadness upon leaving my favorite aunt behind. Train rides, as opposed to planes, were the norm in those days.

The Little Rock Nine

It was September 1957, shortly after we moved to California, that my entire family found ourselves unexpectedly huddled together for comfort around the television. We sat wide-eyed with brimming tears, barely able to cover our mouths to suppress wails of the shock, horror, hurt, and disbelief of what we were seeing.

A lone black teenaged girl walked through a sea of rage, a mob of over four hundred angry white people screaming, yelling, spitting, and taunting her with threats of lynching. She made it back to the bus stop and sat there, poised, silent, allowing tears to fall in their angry midst. Her name was Elizabeth Eckford, and she was the first to attempt to integrate the all-white high school in Little Rock, Central High School. She had ridden the bus and shown up alone before the other black students came to enroll; her family had no phone and she had no way of knowing about the details of their meeting.

I didn't know it at the time, but that previous summer I overheard a phone conversation between my mother and her friend was the first hint that my life would change forever, almost overnight. I had heard my mother say, "Yeah, Daisy Bates is calling around looking for students..." or something to that effect. This conversation stuck with me even though I didn't understand it at the time. It seems as though they were recruiting their best students that summer to integrate the all-white Central High School in the fall.

Some may be amazed to learn this, but other than little vignettes about life experiences, my family never really talked about segregation per se, and most importantly, they never discussed major historical events that were fast brewing the summer of 1957 until they happened. This was the beginning. We knew the Little Rock Nine as individuals. My sister was in classes with most of them, and I was in class with some of their siblings. When we spoke of them it was as individuals, marveling at how they maintained their dignity and showed neither fear nor anger in front of the mob of raging whites. These were nine high school kids, and to whites they were blacks deliberately out of place, an affront to their long-held values that defined racial superiority.

I am limited in my vocabulary even today, to begin to describe or to even relate to Elizabeth Eckford's lone experience on a bus stop facing an angry mob. Ruby Bridges, at six years old, the first black child to integrate the New Orleans school system, did it alone, but she was escorted by law officials. Elizabeth Eckford was truly alone; she had no one. At this stage in my life, generations older, I still could not do it. As my family watched things unfold from the safety of our TV, we remembered some of the individuals for their personalities, their studiousness as well as sense of humor. To see them demonstrate a serious, focused, and self-sacrificial part of themselves was transformational for us. The people I was seeing were not the same people I had known--they had become something other than high school students or young people, they transcended before our eyes to a level unknown to me at the time.

We knew them as Minniejean Brown, Elizabeth Eckford, Ernest Green, Thelma Mothershed, Melba Patillo, Gloria Ray, Terrence Roberts, Jefferson Thomas, and Carlotta Walls. This was who they were when we knew them, but in an instant they became an everlasting part of our nation's history and became as one. They were no longer the people we knew before September 1957, they had ascended to a higher place and would be forever known in American history singularly as The Little Rock Nine. What is important for young people to remember is that these were ordinary high school students who responded to a call and changed America forever. Thank you.

Afterward

Since the time of the Civil Rights Movement, it has become safe to protest. People who represent a movement in these times know that they will not be hosed, beaten, have dogs set upon them, or killed. Many groups, to give their cause strength, frequently liken their cause to the black Civil Rights Movement. This is highly offensive to blacks of my generation who know that there is no comparison. Not only that, the question is asked, if they felt they were equally oppressed and abused, why didn't they join us when we were protesting for our rights?

CPSIA information can be obtained
at www.ICGtesting.com
Printed in the USA
LVOW11s2358240418
574788LV00001B/47/P